"The Devil's Toolbox"
and other sermons
of Clarence K. Stewart

To Dorise Haynes

Clarence K. Stewart

compiled by

Scott Stewart
Susan Wise
Randy Stewart

In memory of our sister

Karen

*who heard Dad's sermons with us
and beheld his Savior before us*

–and–

In honor of our mother

Mary Lou

*whose life is the best sermon we have heard
and whose love is the most Christ-like we have seen*

CONTENTS

Foreword by Randy Stewart 9

EVANGELISM
Communicating the Gospel 15
Fools – Wise and Otherwise 21
Salvation 25
Baseball Diamond Gospel 29
Ashamed – Not Ashamed 33
The Devil's Toolbox 37
The Three Trees of History 45
Stop! Look! Listen! 49
The Agencies of Salvation 53

DISCIPLESHIP
What Do You Weigh? 59
A Principle for Living 63
The Power of Grace 67
The Harp and the Javelin 71
The Friend of God 75
Blueprint for Happy Living 81
Huz and Buz 87
Why Be Good? 91
The Genius of Patience 95
The Bible's Greatest Promise 101
(and my favorite verse of Scripture)

THE LIFE OF CHRIST
Jesus' Birth and the Angels 109
The Greatest Battle Ever Fought 113
His First Message 119
We Would See Jesus 123
What Does Christ See in You? 127
The Hands of Jesus 131
When Impossible Things Become Possible 135
Jesus Weeping on Palm Sunday 139
The Lamb of God 145

***Reminiscing* by Susan Wise**   151

SUFFERING
Fear not! Don't Be Afraid	165
How to Rejoice	171
The Ministry of Encouragement	177
Comfort	181
Loving Promises for Lonely People	185
Rejoice in the Trials of Our Faith	191
Never Lose Heart	193
Remembering Loved Ones	197
Faithful and Flourishing	201

GOD AND THE CHURCH
The Old-Time Religion	211
Worthy	217
God's Toolbox	221
The Promise of God in the Rainbow	225
Blessedness	231
God's Goldmines	235
Nahum's Message	241
The Greatest Love Story	245
The Excitement of Going to Church	251
Eutychus: Sleeping in the Church	257

SPECIAL OCCASIONS
A Father Role Model	265
The Fabulous Father	271
Reflections on Mothers	277
Looking Back and Ahead	281
Walking in the Light	285
Reflections on the Lord's Supper	289
110th Anniversary, First Baptist Church of Pulaski	293
Things I Have Learned as a Minister of the Gospel	297
Final Message	301

***Afterword* by Scott Stewart**   309

FOREWORD

The Stewart family will gather in a few weeks to celebrate the ninetieth birthday of my father. It is a surprise party, and we've taken great lengths to keep it a secret. For one thing, we scheduled the event for June 25th, ten days before his actual birthday. In addition, we joined it to another family festivity. Dad thinks he is coming to Chattanooga for a post-wedding tea for one of his granddaughters, which is true. What he doesn't know is that we will celebrate his birthday as well.

Only one gift will be given to him at the party: this sermon collection. Our plan is to place several copies inside a gift-wrapped box. Once he opens it, he will personally sign a book for every member of the family. I have no doubt that he will be overwhelmed by this tribute. His whole life has revolved around family and preaching. Now, near its sunset, this gift will do the same.

My purpose in this brief introduction is not to summarize my father's accomplishments or his character. That would be a formidable task, indeed. You will learn much about him as you read his sermons, and Susan and Scott will add some details. Hopefully, by the time you reach the end, the sermons themselves will proclaim Dad's life better than I could ever have hoped to do.

What I want to do instead is lay some groundwork, so that you can appreciate Dad's messages and his life all the more. I consider myself qualified for this role for three reasons: I know him as well as anyone; I have typed most of these words myself; and I have spent a quarter of a century as a music minister, always preparing the way for the pastor's sermon. In this foreword, I'm just doing what comes natural.

Clarence Kenneth Stewart was born on July 5, 1926 in Ashland, Kentucky to Thurston and Pauline Stewart. Before his second birthday his father died of tuberculosis, leaving Pauline with three children under the age of five and another in her womb. Never remarrying and never learning to drive, my grandmother relied on the Lord's strength to nurture her children to adulthood and to Christian service. In Dad's case, his call was to the gospel ministry, prefaced by military service, marriage, college, and seminary training.

Fifty-six of my father's sermons have been compiled here, a tribute to his fifty-six years of ministry. They have been transcribed almost verbatim from the notes he handwrote and used from the pulpit. Connecting words (conjunctions, prepositions, and the like) have been inserted to give the feel of an actual sermon rather than a note. Still, each remains in outline form, and thus some details—illustrations, closing remarks, and off-the-script proclamations—are missing. Every sermon in this book, even when read aloud and slowly, takes less than fifteen minutes to complete. In comparison, Dad's messages usually lasted at least twenty-five minutes, so he must have added some substance to his notes while preaching that is not included here.

This notwithstanding, I think these sermon notes give a wonderful glimpse into his style, delivery, and tone. His charm, creativity, and character are also on display. Granted, a good sermon is not always delivered by a good person, but in this case the man and the message line up perfectly. I bear witness that Dad both preached and lived his sermons.

I remember from my childhood and adolescence that my father was a very good preacher. He tried to present the gospel as simply as possible, avoiding controversy and negativity. Until this book was compiled, I took his greatness from the pulpit for granted. Growing up, I heard most of these sermons firsthand (some more than once) and, like most preachers' kids, often failed to give them full attention. "Hearing" them again these past few weeks, I have come to the conclusion that Clarence K. Stewart was an outstanding spokesman for God. He preached a good sermon. In my opinion, he wrote a better sermon than he preached (which is saying a lot). Of course, his best sermon was, and is, his life.

My prayer is this: *May Jesus Christ, not His messenger, receive praise. May the Word of God, not the words of a man, penetrate hearts. May the things of heaven, not those of earth, reign supreme. May actions, not just words, be transformed. And may God's love and peace, not the world's hatred and disillusion, abide forever and ever. Amen.*

I know Dad will approve of this prayer.

Randy Stewart

Evangelism

Communicating the Gospel
Acts chapters 3-5
1 Corinthians 15:1-4 – Romans 10:17

INTRODUCTION

Theologian Rudolf Bultmann has asked the right question for our times: *how do we interpret the gospel to make it relevant to people today?*

The burning question facing church leaders today is, "How do we communicate the gospel to our generation?"

I think first we need to look at the deeper levels of humanity's spiritual and moral need.

1. There are areas of life that are not totally met by social improvement or material affluence.
2. Jesus said, *"What shall it profit a man if he gain the whole world and lose his own soul?"*
3. He said, *"A person's life in no way depends upon the number of his or her possessions."*
4. I detect within people everywhere that there is a hunger to know God.
   a. Some students said recently, "We are guilty, lonely, and empty, afraid of death. We have a longing to know God."
   b. A young girl said to her father, "I want something, but I don't know what."
   c. Erich Fromm writes, "People are alone and lonely for God."
   d. Hobart Mowrer has said that guilt is the central problem of people everywhere.

e. Yes, in the day in which we live, we have reached a certain amount of affluence. Yet we live in a world of hate and loss, war and greed, hunger and disease, and underneath the surface there is guilt and fear.

This was true in the early Church but also today. I believe the gospel of Christ speaks authoritatively to these problems. It has the answer that can change lives.

But how do we communicate the gospel? There are all kinds of ways being used today—internet, radio, television, prayer walks, tracts, newspapers, magazines. We should communicate it like Peter and John did in the early Church in Jerusalem. Their story is recorded in Acts 3-5. Let me review the happenings.

WE CAN COMMUNICATE THE GOSPEL BY SHARING LIKE THEY DID.
1. They proclaimed the good news.
2. They knew well that *faith comes by hearing and hearing by the Word of God* (Romans 10:17).
3. The apostle Peter stood in the midst of paganism, immorality, and social upheaval. He did not proclaim intellectual knowledge, social progress, or works salvation. He proclaimed Jesus Christ, crucified and resurrected.
4. I remind you today that we are proclaimers in the pulpit, in Sunday School, in one-on-one

conversations, and when talking to a group. A witness to others involves praying for them, giving your testimony, or using the Bible to show them how to be saved.
5. A lady in another city said this sometime ago: "We communicate the gospel and then leave the rest to God."

WE CAN COMMUNICATE THE GOSPEL BY LIVING AS THEY DID.

1. They shared the gospel through the holy life that they lived. This is called *lifestyle evangelism*. They lived what they proclaimed.
2. We are told in Acts 4:13 that the people of Jerusalem marveled at Peter and John and took knowledge that they had been with Jesus.
3. Stephen Neill has said that the attitude in the Church today is worldliness instead of holiness.
4. Ephesians 1:4 says, *"Be holy without blame."* 1 Peter 1:15 – *Be holy in all manner of conversation.*
5. Do people see Christ in your personal life? I know of a lost man who said, "My wife's life-testimony led to my salvation."

WE CAN COMMUNICATE THE GOSPEL BY LOVING LIKE THEY DID.

1. A close study of Acts 4-5 reveals that Peter and the apostles loved people. Acts 4:33-37 – They shared their possession with the needy

and hungry. They saw human need and, out of love, met that need.
2. It was said of the early Church: *"See how they love others!"*
3. Today, we must love – not love the ways of people, not love their sin, not love their ugliness and wrong. But we must reach out in love to them that they may be changed by Jesus.
4. Jesus said, *"By this shall people know that you are My disciples, if you love one another."*
5. We need to go to the people who are dying, go with the gospel message, and tell them of the Savior's love, how He came from Heaven above to die on the cross to save them. They may say, "We see real love in you. We want to know your Savior."

WE CAN COMMUNICATE THE GOSPEL BY GETTING EXCITED LIKE THEY DID.

1. At Pentecost, the leaders in Jerusalem thought the disciples were drunk. No, they were filled with God's Spirit! Joy and happiness permeated their lives.
2. The early followers of Christ found something and just had to share it. They didn't have to be told to do it. They did it naturally. In Acts 5:41-42, they went to the temple court and told with enthusiasm and excitement the full message of life.

3. A professional man told me, "One of the greatest experiences in my life was when I told people about Jesus."
4. Today, we note people becoming very excited about many things—dieting, exercising, cures for life-threatening diseases, and sports like football and basketball.
5. I thought, "Why can't we get just as excited about sharing the message of the gospel?" It offers forgiveness and love in the person of Christ.

Fools – Wise and Otherwise
Proverbs 10:21 – 1 Corinthians 3:18

The lips of the righteous nourish many, but fools die for the want of wisdom. – Proverbs 10:21

Do not deceive yourselves. If any of you think you are wise by the standards of this age, you should become fools so that you may become wise.
– 1 Corinthians 3:18

INTRODUCTION

These verses seem almost paradoxical. In the one instance God is speaking from the divine standpoint when He uses *fools*: *"fools die for the want of wisdom."* A fool here is an unthinking, thoughtless, and careless person who is without true understanding; in plain English, a simpleton. God says these fools die. They die in their sins and die under divine judgment for want of wisdom.

In the other passage the word *fools* is used from the standpoint of ungodly men. They look upon those who have been awakened by the Spirit of God in repentance and have put their faith in the Lord Jesus Christ as though they were fools.

So there are unwise fools and there are wise fools. There are fools for the devil and there are fools for Christ's sake. Let's notice some of the fools mentioned in the Bible.

THE ATHEISTIC FOOL (Psalm 14:1)

Examples include Thomas Paine, the Russian astronauts, and the Beatles. How can anyone look at the starry heavens and declare that there is no

God? Can you conceive of a universe without a Mind, an Intelligent Mind?

THE IGNORANT FOOL (Proverbs 1:7)

This fool is closely aligned with the one above. God has spoken in His Word. He has given us instruction. He has shown us the path of life. He warns of judgment to come. He tells us plainly the way of salvation. But some turn away with a sneer and say, "I don't believe that book. I don't understand it." God calls them *fools*, for they *despise wisdom and instruction.*

THE OPINIONATED FOOL (Proverbs 12:15)

This fool will not learn anything because he is not teachable. He is ready to listen, but he is not willing to learn. He is absolutely certain he is right. He shuts his eyes to the teaching of God's Word.

THE MOCKING FOOL (Proverbs 14:9)

This fool says, "I will do as I please." We are living in a day when many are making fun of those who stand for everything pure and holy and will not engage in sin. They scoff and sneer and ridicule. They imagine that they are showing their brilliance and smartness when they *make a mock of sin.* God says they are just revealing what is in their hearts: depravity. Fools, not wise men, mock at sin.

THE SLANDEROUS FOOL (Proverbs 10:18)

There are many of these fools in politics and business. They repeat evil tales. They malign a person's character, ruining his or her reputation.

They may think they are smart, but God calls them fools.

THE COVETOUS FOOL (Luke 12:20)

This person is not prepared for life, death, or eternity. He lays up treasure for himself and is not rich toward God. Our Lord tells us that every person who is more concerned about getting some of the world's goods and making money than about eternal things is a fool.

THE CHRISTLIKE FOOL (1 Corinthians 3:18)

This is the type of fool we need to be. We should be so committed to Christ that the world looks at us as fools. God uses the *foolishness of the cross* to save us. He then uses the "foolishness of discipleship" to spread His love and good news.

Salvation

"Truly, I say to you, unless you are converted and become like children, you will never enter the Kingdom of Heaven." – Matthew 18:3

INTRODUCTION

Actually the word conversion means *to turn around, to change, to turn back.* It means *to repent, to be changed, to be saved, to be regenerated.*

THE **ESSENTIALS** OF CONVERSION

Jesus said in order to get to Heaven you must be converted. This is not man's opinion but God's.

I remind you:

A. All have sinned.

B. We cannot save ourselves.

C. Conversion is essential—necessary.
Jesus called conversion *new birth.* John Wesley preached on this text several times in succession.

A male movie star's need today is not lust, liquor, and luxury but conversion. Today, a female movie star's need is not for men, money, or martinis but conversion. The politician's need is not prestige, power, and pleasure but conversion. The intellectual's need is not for books, brains, and bigness but conversion. The sinner's need is not fame, fun, and fortune but conversion.

Turn yourself around. Jesus said, *"Except ye be converted..."*

THE **ELEMENTS** OF CONVERSION

(Sometimes these terms are misunderstood.)

A. Repentance Is Necessary

   1. John the Baptist: *"Repent for the Kingdom of Heaven is at hand. For godly sorrow leads to repentance."*
   2. Jesus: *"Except you repent, you will likewise perish."*
   3. Peter (Acts 3:19): *"Repent and be converted so that your sins may be wiped out."*
   4. Paul: *"God commands all persons to repent—repent!"*

B. Faith Is Involved

   Paul to the Philippian jailor: *"Believe on the Lord Jesus Christ, and you will be saved."*

C. Grace Is Needed

   John 1:12-13, John 3:16, John 5:24

   Conversion is...

   1. Not of blood
      - Not through the bloodstream.
      - Not through inheritance.
      - Not through birth into a Christian home.
   2. Not through the will of the flesh.
      - Salvation is Savior-centered not man-centered – not just turning over a new leaf.
   3. Not through the will of man.
      - No man can hand you salvation.

THE **EVIDENCES** OF CONVERSION

Evidences there must be! *"A new commandment I give you that you love one another as I have loved you."*

1. A change in your relationship with God. Once a stranger, now a child of God.
2. A change in your relationship with others. *"Love one another."* Illustration: a little girl – "I do know I've been converted. I used to blow my top; now I don't."
3. Uniting with the church.
4. Being baptized.
5. Loving, supporting, and giving to the church.
6. Good works. James: *faith that does not produce works is a dead faith.*
7. Obeying the commands of Christ.
8. Fruits of the Spirit. Galatians 5:22-23 – The fruits of the Spirit will be reflected in your life:

    Love, Joy, Peace, Long-suffering, Gentleness, Goodness, Faith, Meekness, Temperance

Fruit Inspection: *"By their fruit you will know them."*

Baseball Diamond Gospel
Romans 10:1-4

INTRODUCTION

I love baseball. This morning I'm going to use the ball diamond as a parable to portray spiritual truth. When I do this, I am not deviating from the Biblical procedure. Frequently in the Scriptures the writers allude to figures from the athletic field and use them to convey spiritual truths.

1) Paul used the footraces to illustrate the Christian life: *Let us run with patience...*
2) Again, he referred to the sporting field when he said, *"For we wrestle not against flesh and blood but against principalities and powers."*
3) Again, he said, *"So fight! I am not as one who beats the air."* In other words, "I am not shadow-boxing."

Now I want to use the baseball diamond, the bases in particular, to teach spiritual truths, to teach the Christian way.

FIRST BASE REPRESENTS SALVATION

1) This is the initial step. A runner cannot advance unless he goes by first base.
2) In the Christian life, salvation is the first step.
3) This was the burning desire in the heart of Paul for the people of his day. He was not concerned about them being rich and famous. He desired their spiritual redemption.

4) In Paul's day and in ours, the people were going at it the wrong way. They had a zeal for God, but it was not according to knowledge.
5) How do you touch first base? You can't save yourself. You can't become righteous alone.
6) Today, I don't have to belabor the point that we are sinners. Every time we see a bank, we should remember that we are in debt to God. Whenever we see a law enforcement officer, we should recall that we are sinners.
7) In order to receive God's forgiveness and righteousness, you must touch first base. *If you confess with your mouth the Lord Jesus Christ and believe in your heart that God has raised Him from the dead, you will be saved.*

SECOND BASE REPRESENTS JOINING THE CHURCH AND BEING BAPTIZED

1) After one is saved, he or she should affiliate with a church and go to work for the Lord.
2) You can't cut across the pitcher's mound from home plate and go stand on second base. But today many are trying to do this:
   a. Baptized in water but not saved by the blood.
   b. Taking the cup of Communion but not the cup of salvation
   c. Having their names on a church roll but not in the Lamb's Book of Life. Members of a church but not members of the Kingdom of God.
3) Baptism is a picture of salvation, not salvation itself. You should go to first base before being baptized.

THIRD BASE REPRESENTS CHRISTIAN SERVICE

1) Many Christians become converted and then move on to second base and are baptized; then they get a rocking chair, and there they sit on second base.
2) After the Resurrection, Jesus, while cooking for His disciples, said, *"Peter, do you love Me? Feed My sheep."* He was saying, "Do something for Me." Love is expressed in service. Love is crystalized in activity.
3) I admire Paul for what he said after being saved: *"Lord, what will You have me to do?"* He knew that love for Christ was synonymous with service.
4) What can you do for God? Attending church and Bible study, witnessing, etc.

FOURTH BASE REPRESENTS HEAVEN

1) This is the end of the trail.
2) Christ promised that we shall dwell forever in the house of the Lord, in many mansions.
3) When our job is done on earth, we have a home in Heaven.
4) To be absent from the body is to be home with the Lord. We are mere pilgrims here on earth.
5) Going to Heaven is going where Jesus is.
6) Before you can claim this glorious prospect, you must be saved. You must go by first base.

CLOSING

In the seventh game of 1924 World Series, the New York Giants and the Washington Senators were tied in bottom of the ninth inning. There were two outs when Goose Goslin came to bat. Knocking the ball to the outfield fence, Goslin circled the base paths as the fielder chased the ball. He then headed for home, avoided the catcher's tag, and touched home plate.

The hometown crowd was ecstatic, until the umpire threw his thumb in the air and shouted, "He's out! He never touched first base!"

Ashamed – Not Ashamed
Romans 1:16

INTRODUCTION

The Apostle Paul was one of the choicest gospel preachers this world has ever heard. He counted it a great privilege to tell everyone the story of Christ and what the Lord had done for him. He told his story...

...in Jerusalem where Jews opposed him.

...in Asia Minor where they beat him.

...in Athens, the cultural center of the ancient world.

...in Rome, the city which trusted in its military.

Before Paul went to Rome, he wrote a letter to the Christians there. He longed to preach the gospel in this powerful center. He knew that the power of Rome would be against him, but he said in Romans 1:16, *"I am not ashamed of the gospel of Christ. I will proclaim the gospel of Christ against the sin, power, and superstition of Rome."*

But as Paul looked back over his life, he must have thought about many things of which he *was* ashamed:

1) He thought about how he had persecuted Christians and put them to death.
2) He thought about Stephen and how he stood by and watched them stone this good man to death.
3) He thought about how he had made trouble for the Church.

4) He remembered how he had hurt Christ in hurting Christ's followers.

Many things in the past for which he was ashamed haunted him. Now he was to proclaim the gospel of which he was *not* ashamed.

LIKE THE APOSTLE PAUL, WE SHOULD BE ASHAMED OF MANY THINGS.
1) We should be ashamed of our sins.
   a. All of us have sinned.
   b. Sin separates us from God.
2) We should be ashamed of the slow, small progress we have made in the Christian life.
   a. We have grown physically.
   b. We have not developed spiritually. We are spiritual midgets.
   c. We must grow in grace and knowledge.
3) We should be ashamed of the little service we have given to Christ.
4) We should be ashamed that we have not always carried out our good intentions.
   a. We vowed to be faithful.
   b. We vowed to be a tither.
   c. We vowed to read the Bible and pray.

Yes, there are things that haunt us, bother us, which we are ashamed of.

BUT WE CAN SAY WITH PAUL, "I AM NOT ASHAMED OF THE GOSPEL OF CHRIST."
1) We are not ashamed of **the author of the gospel**, Jesus Christ.
   a. The human race did not and could not produce Jesus Christ. He is the only begotten Son of God, virgin-born.

b. Jesus is *the* Person of the gospel. We should not be ashamed of Him.
c. A farmer and his wife from Arkansas sent their son to a university. The son became sophisticated. His dad came to visit him, and the young man was ashamed of his father, ashamed to be seen with his parents.
d. There is no reason on earth for us to be ashamed of Jesus.
   • He is our Everything, our Hero, our Champion.
   • He has given us life.
   • He has given us moral character.
   • He has promised to be with us in death.
2) We are not ashamed of **the message of the gospel**.
   a. It is the only message that has any saving power.
   b. It is better than the message and philosophy of the world.
      • Babylon said, "Eat, drink, and be merry."
      • Rome said, "Pleasure and power will make you happy."
      • Hitler said, "Might makes right."
      • Wall Street says, "Pile up your money."
      • The formalist says, "There is power in ritual."
      • The modernist says, "Every man has in himself a spark of divinity."
      These messages fail, but the gospel never fails.
3) We are not ashamed of **the fruit of the gospel**.
   a. Jesus said, *"By their fruit you shall know them."* The gospel has produced much

fruit. When Christ died, there were only a handful of believers. Now there are millions from every race, tribe, and tongue.
   b. The modernist tells us how to improve the world, but he doesn't tell us that first you must improve the men in the world. How do you change people? The gospel changes them; it produces fruit (results).
4) We are not ashamed of **the goal of the gospel**. Heaven is that goal.
5) We are not ashamed of **the power of the gospel**. 1 Corinthians 15:4 – *He was buried and was raised on the third day.*
6) We are not ashamed of **the promise of the gospel** – He died for our sins!
7) We are not ashamed of **the peace of the gospel**. Ephesians 6:15 – *...and with your feet fitted with the readiness that comes from the gospel of peace.*
8) We are not ashamed of **the fellowship of the gospel**. Philippians 1:5 – *...because of your fellowship in the gospel from the first day until now.*

The Devil's Toolbox
2 Corinthians 11:14 – Job 2:2 – 1 Peter 5:8-9

BACKGROUND

How I was led to develop this message:
1. I began to think of all the ways the Devil was capturing the hearts and minds of kids, youth, and adults.
2. To emphasize the drug culture, I needed some items to use in telling my story. I contacted the sheriff's office, and he gave me several items that had been confiscated. I received marijuana, cocaine, and some drug pills and a pipe used to smoke pot.
3. Following this, a deacon in the church gave me a toolbox. I put there the drug items and other objects that I believed Satan was using to influence people. The message was ready.
4. I have used this sermon in schools, in revivals, and in various churches when I have had the opportunity.
5. An unusual happening occurred when my car, with the toolbox and drugs in the trunk, was stolen while parked near the county courthouse. I became fearful that the law enforcement officers would find the car and find the drugs. I could see the headline: "Baptist Preacher's Car Found with Drugs". The car was found in Alabama. Fortunately, no one had opened the trunk and checked the toolbox that contained the drugs. Needless to say, I breathed a sigh of relief

and quit carrying drugs in this toolbox. I now use substitute drugs to convey part of my message.

INTRODUCTION

The Devil is a real Person. Some people think of Satan as a mythical monster, and therefore they speak of him lightly or seldom. But Satan is the archenemy of God and us.

1. 1 Peter 5:8 – *Be sober, be vigilant, because the Devil, as a roaring lion, walks about, seeking whom he may devour.* He is never still, always stalking us. He is active in the lives of men and women, boys and girls, and young people.
2. The Devil's activity is wholly evil (2 Corinthians 11:14), for *Satan himself masquerades as an angel of light.* He is the *ruler of the world*, the *god of this age*.
3. The Devil is not "the man below" heaping coal into the eternal furnace. He is the original "jet-setter" – active with all people with his latest cause.
4. In Job 2:2ff, when God asked Satan a direct question—*"From whence comest thou?"*—the Devil's answer showed outrageous arrogance. The adversary answered the Lord, *"From going to and fro on the earth and from walking up and down in it."*
5. What a picture! Satan going all over the earth (as the prince and power that he is), wielding his influence and using his message, using tools and instruments, doing his thing at every spot and situation

and with every person he can. He is working in our world systems, education, business, and culture—in the lives of people everywhere—trying to capture their minds and hearts and lead them to eternal hell.

What are some of the ways, tools, or instruments that this adversary, the Devil, is using to lead people to destruction?

THE TASSEL—GAINING OF KNOWLEDGE

(Remember Eve and the tree of knowledge in the Garden of Eden.)

1. Paul wrote: *The wisdom of this world in foolishness before God.*
2. Satan is trying to warp the mind, to manipulate it through Muslim extremism, Freudism, Darwinism, Marxism, and other "isms" of this world. He is doing it in every area – education, the arts, radio, television, music, movies, computers, magazines, and newspapers.
3. Even in high schools, colleges, and other places of higher learning, young people with Christian values have been led astray by the Devil through teachers who have atheistic leanings.

DRUGS

The culture in which we live is filled with drugs of every kind. The Devil is having a heyday in the drug world.

a. Marijuana, cocaine, pills, meth, home-cooked drugs

  b. Liquor – beer, alcoholic beverages
  c. Tobacco products – cigarettes and other products.

  If I had time, I could tell and you could tell of situations where Satan has caused harm in people's lives through drugs. Recall in Romans and Corinthians how Paul tells Christians that it is best to refrain from eating meat offered to idols. This principle applies to the use of drugs.

MONEY AND WEALTH

 1. Paul (1 Timothy 6:10) tells us that money is the root cause of all evil.
 2. We need money for a livelihood. We need money for the necessities of life.
 3. The Devil tries to get individuals to make money their God: to trust in gold, not in God.
  a. He wants you to hoard money.
  b. He wants you to spend it foolishly.
  c. He wants you to rob God.
  d. He wants individuals to make money their goal in life.
 4. Years ago Dr. Charles Albertson was interviewing Cecil Rhodes, a British Empire builder from South Africa. He said to Mr. Rhodes, "You must be the happiest man in the world with all your money." Cecil Rhodes replied, "Good Lord, no! I spent most of my money on lawyers to keep me out of jail and on doctors to keep me alive."

A BOAT—PLEASURE

 Another tool the Devil uses is pleasure. I have pleasure in playing golf. However, the Devil wants you to make pleasure the most important thing in your life and forget about God.

The Bible says in 2 Timothy 3:4 that in the last days men and women would be lovers of pleasure rather than lovers of God. In Titus 3:3 Paul says that people are foolish when they serve divers (many) lusts and pleasures.

Don't make pleasure your God. Take time to worship and serve God regularly.

THE GUN—MURDER

The Devil is so happy when people use the gun to kill.
1. One of the Ten Commandments is *"Thou shalt not kill."*
2. Murder is on the increase in the violent age we live in – in our homes, schools, and cities.
3. Let me remind you that the Devil also wants you to hate and kill people with words or by not caring for others.

A CAR
1. My car that was stolen years ago is a reminder that the Devil is active getting people to break laws by taking things that do not belong to them.
2. *Thou shalt not steal.*

A TRIANGLE—ADULTERY

I am using the triangle to refer to a marriage of a husband and wife broken by the adultery of one party.

1. The Devil is active in broken relationships. The Bible says, *"Thou shalt not commit adultery. Thou shalt not commit fornication."*
2. God intended sex to be meaningful within the husband and wife relationship.
3. There are all types of sexual perverts in society today:
    a. Homosexuals
    b. Lesbians
    c. Sexual perverts who seek out children
4. Billy Graham urges us: "Keep your life wholesome, right, and pure. Abide by the rules."
5. It has always been a mark of a declining civilization to become obsessed by sex.

PORNOGRAPHIC MATERIAL

The Devil is gleeful as he sees the steady stream of perverse, vulgar, and obscene pictures and writings poured out daily like a broken sewer in newspapers, magazines, and books; over the radio and television; and on the internet.

DICE—GAMBLING

How the Devil is using this, even via television, to cause much anguish and heartbreak! There is no command, "Thou shalt not gamble." Does it hurt? Yes! Broken homes and loss of cars and houses result. Gambling makes you depend on luck. God expects you to depend not on chance but to use your skills to earn a living.

OLD SHOE TONGUE

The Devil influences people to lie, to bear false witness. The use of the tongue can be wicked. The Bible says, *"Do not bear false witness against others. Keep your tongue from evil."* Proverbs 17:20 says, *"He that hath a perverse tongue falleth into mischief, malicious gossip, and lying."* The Bible also says, *"Let no corrupt communication proceed out of your mouth."*

CLOSING

Perhaps you could mention other tools the Devil is using to capture the hearts, minds, and lives of people.

Let me close this message by telling you weapons we can use against the Devil's ways:

1. One needs to know God by trusting Jesus Christ as Savior.
2. James 4:7 – *Submit yourself to God. Resist the Devil, and he will flee from you.*
3. Paul (Romans 12:2): *Don't let the Devil squeeze you into his way.*
4. Remember, when Jesus was tempted, He used the Word of God.
5. Let's look at Ephesians 6:10-18 – *Put on the whole armor of God, that you may stand against the wiles of the Devil.*
    a. The girdle or belt – Gird yourself with TRUTH. Jesus said, *"I am the way, the truth, and the life."*
    b. The breastplate protected the vital organs. Paul says that RIGHTEOUSNESS is the Christian's breastplate.

c. Have your feet shod with the preparation of the GOSPEL. Be ready to defend and declare the gospel.
d. The shield of FAITH, to stop the Devil's attack.
e. The sword of the Spirit, which is the WORD OF GOD. Use the written Word of God that Jesus used against Satan when tempted.
f. Pray always in every phase of a conflict with the Devil. We all must enlist the aid of our all-powerful God.

God will give us the strength to resist. However, in our times of weakness, when we may give in and commit sins or do wrong, remember 1 John 1:9 – *If we confess our sins, He is faithful and just to forgive us our sins and to cleanse us from all unrighteousness.*

The Three Trees of History
Genesis 2:16-17 – 1 Peter 2:24
Revelation 2:7, 22:14

INTRODUCTION

You will recognize that the word "tree" occurs in each of these verses, although each deals with a different tree. God gathers the entire history of the human race around three trees.

Henry van Dyke, in his collection of stories entitled *The Valley of Vision,* has one story called "A Sanctuary of Trees". In this moving story, a man has a dream in which his soul seems to appear before God in Heaven. The Lord says to the man, "How did you come hither?" The man answers, "By Christ's way, by the way of the tree."

This striking statement suggests a profound truth. It is a statement which, in itself, contains the essence of the whole drama of salvation, of man's fall and redemption.

The phrase "by the way of the tree" calls to mind three trees of the Bible. As we look at them and understand their meaning, we can clearly see God's plan and provision for the redemption of mankind.

THE TREE OF TEMPTATION—Genesis 2:16-17

God created man and breathed into his nostrils the breath of life, and man became a living being. Genesis 2 tells us that God planted a garden in Eden and caused the tree of knowledge of good and evil to grow in the midst of the garden. God then created woman to be a helpmate to the man.

The tempter, in the form of a serpent, induced the woman to doubt and disobey God's commandment.

The Lord confronted the guilty pair with their disobedience. The man laid the blame on the woman. The woman blamed the serpent. The Lord pronounced a curse upon the serpent and punishment upon the man and woman for their disobedience and sin. Adam and Eve were driven out of the garden, and the Lord placed cherubim and a flaming sword to guard the tree of life. They were banished from the presence of God. Their communion and fellowship with God was lost.

Ever since then, all men and women have been involved in the sin, guilt, and punishment of our first parents. All have eaten of the forbidden fruit of the tree of temptation. All have been involved in the fall of man. Romans 3:22-23 – *For there is no distinction; since all have sinned and fallen short of the glory of God.*

THE TREE OF REDEMPTION—1 Peter 2:24

The cross of Christ is referred to as a tree in several places in the New Testament:

Acts 5:30 – Peter to the Jewish council: *"God raised up Jesus that you hanged on a tree."*

Acts 13:29 – Paul in Antioch of Pisidia: *"They took Him down from the tree."*

Galatians 3:13 – Christ *"became a curse for us...by hanging on a tree."*

1 Peter 2:24 – *"He Himself bore our sins in His body on the tree."*

The cross of Christ is the tree of man's redemption. It was the manner of His death. It was also the meaning of His death. The Bible declares this truth many times. (See Romans 5:8, 1 Timothy 1:15. 1 Peter 1:18-19, 2 Corinthians 5:21.)

THE TREE OF LIFE—Revelation 2:7, 22:14

The book of Revelation contains the following references to the tree of life:

>**Revelation 2:7** – *To the one who is victorious, I will give the right to eat from the tree of life, which is in the paradise of God.*
>
>**Revelation 22:1-2** – *On each side of the river stood the tree of life...*
>
>**Revelation 22:14** – *Blessed are those who wash their robes, that they may have the right to the tree of life and may go through the gates into the city.*

As the Garden of Eden had its flowing river and its tree of life, so the paradise of God has its flowing river and its tree of life – life abundant, life eternal, life forevermore. Through the tree of redemption (the cross of Christ), God has abolished the curse of the tree of temptation. "Paradise Lost" has been restored, and with it the tree of life. It is now "Paradise Regained", where His redeemed people might enjoy the pleasure of His presence forever. Revelation 22:1-5 gives us a glorious description of that city.

We may be sure that all who safely reach the paradise of God, all who share the light and glory of the City of God, when the Lord asks the question, "How did you come hither?," will answer, "By Christ's way, by the way of the tree."

Stop! Look! Listen!
Roman 6:12 – John 3:14 – John 16:7

INTRODUCTION

In 1912 a contest was held offering $3500 for a slogan to be put at railroad crossings. The contest was won by Ralph R. Upton, a lecturer on public safety, who submitted the now famous words: "Stop! Look! Listen!"

These words saved many lives at railroad crossings. However, these imperatives—*Stop! Look! Listen!*—can be used in each of our lives. We have to face many dangerous situations in life. Moral and spiritual forces may collide, bringing havoc and wreckage to life. The world, the flesh, and the Devil seek to trap us and lead us astray.

Today, let us clothe "Stop! Look! Listen!" with a spiritual meaning and with the Word of God and use them to help guide us to spiritual safety.

STOP!

Romans 6:12 – *Therefore do not let sin reign in your bodies.*

1. Sin is missing the mark.
2. Sinners by nature choose to practice sin.
3. James writes: *"He that knoweth to do right and doeth it not, it is sin."*
4. Modern people do not like to be told to stop sinning.
5. "Stop!" smacks of being outdated, as religious fanaticism.
6. Yet we would not hesitate to use the word "stop" in the presence of great danger:

       A. A little child ready to dart into a busy highway
       B. A rattlesnake ready to strike a companion
7. The Bible does not hesitate to insist that we stop drifting into sin.
       A. Paul: *"Do not let sin reign in your bodies."*
       B. Paul: *"Do not be deceived. God is not mocked. Whatever a man sows, he will reap."*
       C. James: *"Sin, when it is finished, brings death."*
8. Sin, sown like a seed, grows and grows to be a harvest of iniquity.
       A. Samson
       B. David
       C. Young adults who are drinking and using pornography

What about you? Don't let sin reign.

LOOK!

1. Scripture passages:
       A. Isaiah 45:22 – *Look unto Me, and be ye saved, all the ends of the earth.*
       B. Psalms – *They looked to Him and were enlightened.*
       C. John the Baptist – *Behold (Look!), the Lamb of God!*
       D. John 3:14 – *As Moses lifted up the serpent in the wilderness, even so the Son of Man must be lifted up.*
2. When people looked at Jesus, they saw the forgiveness of God etched in human flesh.
3. A look at Jesus in faith provides salvation.

4. To look at His love is to be cheered in moments of despair.
5. To look at His courage is to be heartened in moments of danger.
6. To look at His patience is to be strengthened in time of frustration.

> *Turn your eyes upon Jesus,*
> *Look full in His wonderful face,*
> *And the things of earth will grow strangely dim*
> *In the light of His glory and grace.*

7. Charles Haddon Spurgeon: "I looked and I lived." Indeed, the New Testament defines the whole Christian life in this way when it says, *"Let us run with patience the race set before us, looking unto Jesus, the author and finisher of our faith."*
8. Look and live, my brother! Look to Jesus now and live.

LISTEN!

1. Before Jesus died, He told His disciples that He was going away. *"When I go away, do not fear. I will send the Spirit."*
2. After His death, Jesus did not become merely a memory to those who had known Him.
3. In a John Masefield play, *The Trial of Jesus*, one scene pictures the wife of Pilate talking with the Roman centurion.

   CENTURION: Did you see Jesus die in humility?
   PILATE'S WIFE: Do you think he is dead?
   CENTURION: No, lady, I don't.
   PILATE'S WIFE: Then where is he?

CENTURION: Let loose in the world, lady, where neither Roman nor Jew can stop the truth.

4. So it is today. His message of truth is let loose in the world. The prophet speaks, *"You shall hear My voice over the shoulder, saying, 'This is the way; walk ye in it.'"* Only when we are listening for our Lord will we be guided to make the right decision.
5. You must listen to the call of God.
   A. He wants to save you.
   B. He wants to guide you.
   C. He wants your life to be surrendered to Him.

CLOSING

Here again is this simple formula:

1. **Stop** your involvement with sin.
2. **Look** to the Savior and believe.
3. **Listen** to God speak to you now.

God, through His Spirit, is saying, "Come! Come now!"

The Agencies in Salvation
Isaiah 59:1,16

INTRODUCTION

One of the problems in our world is communication: defining what you mean. An example of this is the definition of the word *salvation*. Webster's Dictionary states that the definition of salvation is this:

1) The process of being saved from any physical, mental, social, or spiritual situation.
2) In theological terms, it means deliverance from sin and its penalty.

Salvation in the Bible has several meanings. It may mean *to save, to keep safe, to rescue or deliver from danger or destruction.* For Israel throughout the Old Testament, it meant deliverance from oppression or bondage.

a. Moses was the leader in delivering and rescuing the children of Israel held in bondage.
b. Joshua continued the process of leading as they possessed the land of Canaan.
c. During the period of the judges, Gideon, Samson, and others delivered or rescued Israel from enemies.
d. During the times when kings ruled, David and other kings became the ones who rescued the people from danger and delivered them.
e. In the period when the prophet Isaiah lived and spoke God's message, after

declaring that Israel had sinned and transgressed God's holy Law again and again, he declared: *"The Lord was the only one who could deliver and save you"* (59:1). Verse sixteen reads: *The Lord saw their evil and brought their salvation. Their deliverance, their hope was in the Lord God.*

From this text, let me proclaim tonight three great truths.

MAN CANNOT SAVE MAN

1) Cain tried his own way, trying to save himself.
2) Pre-Judaism was a crude and primitive example of this teaching. It placed the person's ability to save on man. It was man trying to save man.
3) In the days when Jesus walked among them, the Jews had found in the Law 613 distinct commandments to keep – man trying to save man.
4) In our world today it is the same.
    a. The Muslims say, "Fast, pray, and give allegiance to Mohammad, and you will be saved."
    b. In Hinduism, salvation is obtained by overcoming evil.
    c. In the religious world today there are all kinds of groups and "isms" that proclaim how a good life, works, keeping the Law, etc. saves. This is man trying to save man.
    d. Some individuals have claimed that they are the Messiah. Again, this is man trying to save man.

GOD ALONE CAN SAVE MAN

1) Here we have the important addition of the divine agent. God is at work saving man. Isaiah declares it. As Jonah cried out, *"Salvation is of the Lord."*
2) God is the Redeemer, blazoned on the pages of the Old and New Testaments.
3) God saves through His Son Jesus Christ.
4) God can save because He is the Author and Finisher of salvation.
5) While in school in Louisville, Kentucky, I had a professor who declared the salvation story this way: "God declares the inspired truth, revealed in His Holy Word, that man is sinful, God is holy, and that Jesus died, was buried, arose, ascended to Heaven, and is coming again. Then the Holy Spirit takes these truths of Scripture and convicts the person of sin and unrighteousness, warns him or her of judgment, and leads that person into a glorious salvation experience." Thus God is the divine One who brings salvation.

GOD DOES USE MAN TO SAVE MAN

1) God has elected to use human agencies to point men, women, youth, boys, and girls to Jesus Christ.
2) God does the saving, but He allows us who know Him to show others the way.
   a. In Israel's deliverance from bondage, He used Moses.
   b. When Simon Peter was saved, God used his brother Andrew to show the way.
   c. God often uses the testimony of a Christian or the witness of a friend to bring a person to Christ.

    d. Sometimes a crisis experience or a situation through which God speaks turns the person to salvation in Christ.
3) God is indeed in the midst of men saving men. He uses individuals to share the message with them.
4) God uses the Church, the fellowship of believers, and Sunday School teachers to get the message to sinners, and then God does the saving.
5) I want you to remember: Stay close to God. Share your faith and bring people to God. Be the people of God by bringing people to God through Jesus Christ.

Discipleship

What Do You Weigh?
Daniel 5:24-28 – Job 31:6

INTRODUCTION

Several years ago I was at Coney Island, an amusement park near Cincinnati, Ohio. As I walked up and down this midway, I noticed several people gazing at a large scale. My attention focused on a sign which said, "I Can Guess Your Weight." The sign went on to say that if the young attendant at the scale did not guess your weight within five pounds, you would win a prize. Little people, middle-sized people, and big people took their turns. I was amazed at how accurate the young man was. He guessed nine out of ten correctly.

This story calls to my mind two passages of Scripture. I know you will remember the first passage in Daniel 5. The king of Babylon gave a great feast. Before the eyes of his astonished guests, a part of a hand came from nowhere and wrote these four words on the wall: *Mene, Mene, Tekel, Upharsin.* Daniel interpreted the word "Tekel" to mean, *"Thou art weighed in the balances and art found wanting."*

The other verse, Job 31:6, is one that is filled with such a great message for us: *"Let me be weighed in an even balance, that God may know mine integrity."* Job was talking to his so-called friends and comforters. They had been interpreting his disasters as punishment for his disobedience and sins. Job's defense was this magnificent statement. *"Let God weigh me in an even balance"* —that is, in scales that are perfectly balanced— *"and both you and God can know my integrity."*

From these two passages, let us consider

three sets of scales or balances that we would do well to always keep in mind.

WHAT DO YOU WEIGH IN YOUR OWN SCALES?

1. This scale is individual and belongs to you alone.
2. No one can see the face of this scale except you.
3. There are many things about you that no one else knows.
4. You know yourself better than anyone.
5. What do you weigh in your own private scales?
6. Paul said, *"Let a man examine himself."*
    a. What are the desires of your heart?
    b. What are the things for which you yearn in life?
    c. What is the purpose of your life?
    d. What are the thoughts in your life? Are they ugly and vulgar or pure and lovely? Someone has said, "Tell me what your thoughts are, and I'll tell you what kind of person you are."

WHAT DO YOU WEIGH IN THE SCALES OF OTHERS?

1. These are scales that you cannot see. The face is turned the other way.
2. These scales are more important than you sometimes think. Your influence is sacred. No Christian has the right to say, "I don't care what people say about me."
3. Paul realized the importance of these scales.

He urged us to *adorn the doctrine of the gospel.* He knew the importance of making the Christian life so beautiful that others would want what we have.
4. What do you weigh in the scales of other people?
    a. Are people better because of your life?
    b. Are they better off because they know you?
    c. *For none of us lives to himself, and no man dies to himself* (Romans 14:7).
    d. Remember these words from a hymn: "Your life's a book before their eyes." Set an example!

WHAT DO YOU WEIGH IN THE SCALES OF GOD?

1. These are the scales that Job talked about.
2. His desire was that God would weigh him on an even balance so that He would know his integrity.
3. We should pray Job's prayer.
4. If God were to put what we are today on one side of His balance and place on the other side what He expects us to be, what would be the measure of that scale?
5. God's scale weighs our integrity, courage, honesty, sincerity, earnestness, zeal for kingdom work, and faith.
6. What do you weigh in God's scales?

A Principle for Living
Matthew 6:25-34

INTRODUCTION

In this passage, Jesus talks about: (1) the nature of worry, (2) the impropriety of worry, and (3) overcoming worry.

What principle are you living?

SOME PEOPLE ARE LIVING ON **THE PRINCIPLE OF DRIFT**.

Like a log in the river, they are drifting along with the tide. There are many people who live this way. They have no intention, no purpose, no direction. They simply let life carry them along wherever it will.

Some listening to me today have no purpose, no direction, and no goal. You are going nowhere. Some of you adults are like this. Some of you youth are like this. If your life has no aim, no meaning, and no end in view—if you are just drifting—then Jesus has a word for you.

THERE ARE OTHERS WHO DEPEND ON **THE PRINCIPLE OF LUCK**.

They hope the stars will shine on them, that good fortune will attend their way, that somehow circumstances will combine to bless them with all they need and more. Are you living like that?

OTHERS TAKE AS THEIR MOTTO FOR LIFE **THE PRINCIPLE OF STRUGGLE**.

From the beginning of life to the end, they focus on how they struggle:
- A. They struggle to be good.
- B. They struggle to be successful.
- C. They struggle to be famous.
- D. They struggle to be rich.
- E. They struggle to be powerful.
- F. They struggle to be happy.

The Bible and Jesus enunciate another kind of principle for living.

Here it is...

SEEK FIRST **THE PRINCIPLE OF THE KINGDOM OF GOD**.

This truth is announced in the Old Testament.
- A. Isaiah 55: 6-7 – *Seek the Lord while He may be found; call upon Him while He is near. Let the wicked forsake his way and the unrighteous man his thoughts; and let him return to the Lord, and He will have compassion on him, and to our God.*
- B. Jeremiah 29:13 – *And you shall seek Me and find Me when you shall search for Me with all your heart.*
- C. 2 Chronicles 15:2 – *The Lord is with you while you are with Him, and if you seek Him, He will let you find Him.*

Am I talking to someone who has been drifting, someone who has depended on luck, someone who has been struggling and getting nowhere? Jesus suggests a new formula for living: "Go! Put God first! Seek first the kingdom of God."

Whatever else this says, it tells us that the man or woman who does not take God seriously will never find any meaning, any satisfaction, any fullness in his or her Christian experience. A religion or a Christian life which is not based on a search, a longing, a thirst, and a need for God is nothing. You will seek Him when you know you need Him, when you place a value on Him, when you sense that you are not adequate yourself.

If you are not a Christian this morning, you need Him. You need Him to forgive your sins, to remake your life. Seek and you shall find.

And if you are a Christian this morning, you need Him too. Oh, how you need Him to guide you through your life day by day, to chart your course! We cannot chart our own course. We must seek His Lordship.

This is the principle that Jesus suggests to us. Take God seriously enough to long for Him, to seek Him, to reach out to Him, and you will have taken the first step to discovering real life and real peace.

THERE IS **A PRIORITY FOR LIVING** IN THIS WORD OF JESUS.

1. Seek first the kingdom of God. We need to get our priorities right.
2. Think for a moment about the following things in your life: money, happiness, your faith, your job, your family, your automobile, your sport, your hobby. Now, be honest. Which will come first?

3. Now list them in the order of priority they should have for you. Oh, I don't mean the order *you* think they should be. Put them in the order they really should be... in God's kingdom.

The Power of Grace
Titus 2:11-12

INTRODUCTION

Many errors in our world come from one-sidedness. We tend to see one aspect of truth and proclaim it as the whole. An interesting illustration concerns one of the most common and, at the same time, most beautiful words in the Christian vocabulary. The word is *grace*. We testify about the grace of God and sing about it. We write definitions of it. Yet too often we don't understand grace.

The New Testament word *grace* has a distinct beauty. It's the Greek word *charis*. In classical Greek it means beauty, charm, attractiveness. Its meaning was extended to mean favor, kindness, and gratitude—unmerited favor. When New Testament writers took over the term *grace*, they used it to describe the spontaneous, beautiful, unearned love of God in Christ to sinners and the operation of that love in the lives of Christians.

Today we can learn something about grace by using the letters of the English word as an acrostic:

1. The "**G**" stands for **God**, the source of grace. 1 Peter 5:10 – *May the God of all grace who hath called us into His eternal glory by Christ Jesus...make you perfect, establish, strengthen, and settle you.*
2. The "**R**" means **redemption**, the purpose of grace. Ephesians 1:7 – *In whom we have redemption through His blood, the forgiveness of sins, according to the riches of His grace.*

3. "**A**" is for **abundance**, the measure of grace. 2 Corinthians 9:8 – *God is able to make all grace abound toward you.*
4. "**C**" points to **Christ**, the mediation of grace. 2 Corinthians 8:9 – *For you know the grace of our Lord Jesus Christ, that, though He was rich, yet for your sakes He became poor, that you through His poverty might be rich.*
5. "**E**" speaks of **eternity**, the culmination of grace. Romans 5:20-21 – *But where sin abounded, grace did much more abound; that as sin hath reigned unto death, even so might grace reign through righteousness unto eternal life in Jesus Christ our Lord.*

Yet with all these truths about grace, many still stumble over its meaning because they see only one side. Grace is usually defined as the unmerited favor or mercy of God. Salvation is all of grace and none of works. But to stop at justification is to miss the complete thrust of the gospel. We are justified by God's grace in order that we may be purified in grace to full living. Grace not only provides pardon; it also provides power for righteousness. It is not only saving grace for a forgiven past; it is sanctifying grace for a transformed present and future.

Grace is not one-sided. It has many sides. One of the finest Biblical statements of this many-sided grace is preserved in Titus 2:11-14. Note here the entire scope of God's grace.

IT IS GRACE THAT SOUGHT US

1. vs. 11 – *Grace hath appeared to all men.*

2. When we were far away from God, His grace pursued us. His grace hounded us.
3. This is the grace that comes to the heart before the heart turns to the Savior.
4. God's grace came seeking after Adam sinned. He has been trying to show His grace ever since. He came seeking, convicting, calling, wooing.

IT IS GRACE THAT SAVES US
1. vs. 11 – *Grace brings salvation.*
   vs. 14 – *He gave Himself for us that He might redeem us from all iniquity.*
2. Grace that pardoned us from all our sins.
3. Paul, chief of all sinners: *"I am what I am by the grace of God."*

IT IS GRACE THAT SANCTIFIES US
1. vs. 12 – Grace helps us live as Christians by teaching us.
2. It is grace that helps us to:
   a. Renounce ungodliness
   b. Renounce earthly lust
   c. *Live soberly and righteously in this present world*
3. After we trust Christ as Savior, God's grace does not stop. It continues with us.
   a. When we are tempted to go the world's way, God provides grace to say "no".
   b. When those who are ungodly seek to influence us to pursue the godless way, God gives grace to say "no" and prompts and encourages us to live soberly, righteously, and godly.

IT IS GRACE THAT SUSTAINS US

    1. vs. 14 – Grace helps us keep going when hard knocks come our way.
    2. How often in life the hurts and losses cause us to lose heart and get our own eyes off Christ, and we falter in our own work for our Lord! Things that cause us to wane in our allegiance:
        a. disappointment in others
        b. disabilities and sickness
        c. death – grace to live and grace to die

In all of these, it is God's grace that sustains and preserves us to be zealous in our work for Him and to constantly look for the blessed hope of the coming of Jesus.

IT IS GRACE THAT IS SUFFICIENT

    1. From the cradle to the grave, His grace is sufficient.
    2. In good times and bad times, God's sufficiency is felt.
    3. From the beginning of life to the end of life, His grace satisfies.

CLOSING

The many sides of grace: sought us, saves us, sanctifies us, sustains us, is sufficient for us.

Are you today in need of God's grace?

    1. Is your sin under condemnation?
    2. Are you drifting as a Christian?
    3. Are the hurts of life rushing in on you?

Add God's grace to your life. His grace is sufficient for all of life. It is sufficient until we see Jesus.

The Harp and the Javelin
1 Samuel 18:10-11

INTRODUCTION

In today's world, two powers are at our disposal. One is the power of the javelin or spear which typifies violence, force, physical strength, hatred, and bitterness. The other is the power of music, symbolizing love and kindness. Both choices are available. Which one we choose determines the kind of world we live in. Which one we choose also determines the kind of person we become.

As Christians, we aim for growth and maturity. We are dissatisfied to stay on the level at which we found Christ. We must be careful, in our march toward spiritual maturity, not to use power for spiritual maturity. It is not power of force that aids in Christian development. It is the power of submission, the strength of kindness.

Today, singing and music are at the heart of our worship. Can you imagine coming to church and not singing? The Bible is filled with examples of people of God who broke out in song:

1) As Moses led the children of Israel across the Red Sea, they broke out in song.
2) The night Jesus was born, the angels broke out into singing.
3) The night Paul and Silas were in prison, they sang praises to God. (Perhaps we would have complained or would have been in a state of depression.)
4) In the book of Revelation, it says that they sang a new song (5:9).

From Genesis to Revelation there is a continuing song. Music is at the heart of our faith in God.

DAVID HELD IN HIS HAND THE POWER OF THE HARP.

I want to go back now to the days when Saul was King of Israel. He was a moody person—one day depressed, the next day elated. Some days he felt good and could do almost anything, but other days he walked in the valley of depression.

His advisors said, "We should do something about these periods of depression that come on Saul. Maybe we can employ a musician."

So they secured a young man by the name of David, a sheepherder, a poet, and a singer. David would play and sing for Saul, and the king would feel better.

Music has a power to affect our emotions and moods. Radio and stereo music changes moods. Music has the ability to evoke memories that long have been dormant in our mind—western songs like *Cool, Cool Water* and *Home on the Range*; home songs like *My Old Kentucky Home*; patriotic songs such as *America, the Beautiful.* Music has a power to bring back feelings of nostalgia. Music also has the power to make us sad. *Precious Memories* evokes a feeling of sadness and loneliness. But music also has the power to fill our hearts with warmth, love, and kindness. We Christians all love religious music. It moves, it stirs, it challenges.

Music has tremendous potential to touch and move us emotionally, and that's why they brought David into the palace to play for Saul. But there came a day when the music stopped.

There's always a danger that a time will come when the music stops for you and me—in our homes, in our marriages, in our churches, in our personal lives. I don't mean we'll stop singing hymns, but we'll stop having music and joy in our hearts.

There's the danger that music will stop in our home and that music will stop in our communities, in our nation, or in our relationships with others.

KING SAUL HELD IN HIS HAND THE POWER OF THE JAVELIN

There was a day when the music stopped as far as the relationship of Saul and David was concerned, and it did so out of jealousy. Here's how it happened:

- A giant, Goliath, in the Philistine army challenged the Israelites by saying, "I'll fight any man you send me." No one volunteered except David. His father had sent him to visit his brothers in the army, maybe to take food and gifts. He had no armor, sword, or javelin. He was a harp-playing teenager who watched sheep.
- David went to the creek bed and picked up five smooth stones. Only one was needed. He let go with such tremendous force that the stone embedded itself in the giant's forehead. He fell to the ground. David finished the job.
- After the great military victory, there was a parade with much singing and happiness. They made up a new song, beautiful to the ears of David but not to Saul: "Saul has slain his thousands. David has slain his ten-thousands."

- Saul was jealous. Hatred and bitterness developed toward David. Saul thought, "He will take my throne." So Saul decided to get rid of David.
- The next time David came into his room to play for him, Saul reached for the spear, pulled it back, and threw it at David, meaning to pin him against the wall.

Today at your disposal and at my disposal is the power of the javelin, which King Saul held in his hand and which people today use. And there's also the power of the harp, which David held in his hand. In our imagination, we see the two at a standoff there in the palace as David plays his harp and as Saul fingers the javelin. Somehow the spirit of greed, jealousy, hatred, and bitterness got the upper hand. The javelin won, and the music stopped.

And the music will stop—in your life and mine, in your marriage and mine, in your family and mine, in your church, on your job and mine—whenever we stoop to pick up the javelin.

The Friend of God
James 3:23

INTRODUCTION

Who is the poorest man on earth? He is the man who has no friends. I would hate to be forced to say, "I don't have a friend in the world." Friendship is a beautiful and blessed thing. When you find a true friend, you have a pearl of great price.

Someone asked a great author for the secret of his success, and he replied, "I had a friend." Many of us can say the same. But what is a friend?

Proverbs 18:24 – *There are friends who pretend to be friends, but there is a friend who sticks closer than a brother.*

Aristotle: "A true friend is one soul in two bodies." He is one who knows all about you and still loves you. He is one who comes in when others go out.

In the Bible, David and Jonathan were great friends. When Jonathan's father, Saul, tried to kill David, Jonathan helped his friend David to escape. Ruth and Naomi were great friends. They shared sorrows and joys together.

But Jesus Christ is the greatest friend of all. John 15:13-15 – *Greater love has no one than this: to lay down one's life for his friends. You are My friends if you do what I command you. I no longer call you servants, because a servant does not know his master's business. Instead, I have called you friends, for everything that I have learned from My Father I have made known to you.*

James writes: *Now Abraham believed God ...and he was called the friend of God"* (2:23). What a wonderful title! And the beautiful thing about it is that all of us can be friends of God, the greatest Friend.

This morning I want to suggest several truths about a friend of God.

A FRIEND OF GOD HAS BEEN REDEEMED

    1) The one who has never trusted God is still in his sin. He is at enmity with God. The Bible calls that person a sinner.
    2) The only way that one can be a friend of God is to repent and believe in Jesus as Savior. That's the way Paul became a friend of God.
    3) I have preached and witnessed to thousands of people and explained that the only way to become a friend of God is to trust His only begotten Son Jesus Christ.
    4) Some try their own way, such as good works and keeping the Law. But when one gives his heart to Jesus Christ, he becomes a child of God and a friend of God.

AFTER BECOMING A FRIEND OF GOD, THE BELIEVER WILL HAVE A DESIRE TO READ AND KNOW ABOUT GOD

    1) Sometime ago I heard about a young woman who was engaged to a young man overseas and who received a letter from him. It was a letter from the one she planned to marry. She

read it once, then again and again. Each word had meaning to her.
2) The Bible is God's letter to you and me. How do you treat it? Do you neglect it? It is full of good things that God has put there to bless you. The Bible contains light to direct you, food to support you, and comfort to cheer you. To the discouraged, the Bible has a message of hope. To those who are distressed by the storms of life, the Bible is an anchor sure and steadfast.
3) As a friend of God, read it, study it, live it. It will make you a better friend to Him.

A FRIEND OF GOD TALKS TO GOD

1) This means that we should be praying people.
2) The Bible reminds us that the effectual praying of God's people avails much.
3) When I pastored in Indiana during my seminary days, the telephone systems contained telephones on party lines. People would get on the line and talk about family problems, trouble with the children, and health situations. The elderly in the community communicated with others on the telephone, talking about their needs.
4) Our telephone as a friend of God is prayer. Communicate with Him. Tell Him about your need and the need of others.
5) Jesus said: *"And I will do whatever you ask in My name, so that the Father may be glorified in the Son. You may ask Me for anything in My name, and I will do it."*
6) Our praying penetrates the hearts we cannot open, shields those we cannot

guard, teaches where we cannot speak, comforts where our hearts have no power to soothe, follows the steps of our friends during trials and hurts, and lifts the burdens with an unseen hand. Friends must talk to God, our Friend, for answers.
7) God is our Friend, on the end of our line. If you want to keep close to Him, He will listen when you pray.

A FRIEND OF GOD WILL BE WILLING TO SERVE HIM AND EVEN SACRIFICE FOR HIM

1) *For we are God's handiwork, created in Christ Jesus to do good works, which God prepared in advance for us to do* (Ephesians 2:10).
2) Abraham served and sacrificed for God, his Friend.
3) Dr. Bill Wallace in 1935 went to China and gave fifteen years in healing bodies and winning people to Christ. In 1950 he was killed by the Chinese Communists.
4) Remember the words of the hymn: *The longer I serve Him, the sweeter He grows.*

A FRIEND OF GOD DESIRES TO HAVE FELLOWSHIP WITH GOD IN WORSHIP

1) Yes, we all enjoy fellowship with our friends.
2) How true this ought to be with our wonderful Friend—God's Son, Jesus Christ! That's what worship is all about.
3) Paul, the greatest apostle, gave these instructions to Christians: *Forsake not the assembling of yourselves together for worship and fellowship with God's people.*

4) As we come to worship, God our Friend is there to challenge us, to energize us, to fellowship with us. Then we can go out and tell others, "How great a Friend our God is!"

Blueprint for Happy Living
Matthew 5:1-12

INTRODUCTION

Thomas Jefferson, the brain behind the Declaration of Independence, in the last phrase of that document, declared in this new government that all people have the right to life, liberty, and the pursuit of happiness. However, many people miss happiness. Why? Because they pursue it the wrong way:

a. Pleasure
b. Wealth, money
c. Popularity
d. Personality

But happiness cannot be purchased with a price.

Jesus taught us how to be happy. On the night of His crucifixion, He said, *"These things have I spoken unto you that My joy may be in you, and that your joy may be full."* His message in His ministry was, "Surrender your life to Me as Savior and Lord. Then you will first find happiness and joy in your life. This is where happiness begins."

However, Jesus taught additional ways of being happy. One day in the life of His ministry, He gathered His disciples around Him and gave them a course on happy living. Let us look at these eternal words from Matthew, chapter 5.

A HAPPY PERSON IS **HUMBLE** (verses 3-5)

1. vs. 3 – This verse teaches humility. A proud spirit cannot gain true happiness.

2. Jesus is our example in humility. He humbled Himself.
3. The publican in the Temple exhibited humility, not the Pharisee.
4. vs. 4 – One who is mourning over the loss of a loved one becomes humble and submissive to the Lord's will.
5. *God resists the proud and gives grace to the humble. Humble yourselves under the mighty hand of God that He may exalt you in due time* (1 Peter 5:5-6).
6. vs. 5 – Meek does not mean weak. It means the meek are ready to obey God and follow His guidance.
7. Dr. Henry Overstreet, in his book *The Mind Goes Forth*, emphasizes that people are going to have to lose their pride if they are going to be happy.

A HAPPY PERSON WILL BE **HOLY** (verses 6,8)

1. These two verses say that a sinful person cannot be a happy person.
2. Psychologists are continually warning us concerning the horrible toll a wrong life and guilt from a life not lived right has on us.
3. Not living the right kind of life is reflected in unhappiness.
4. Living a clean and pure life will bring satisfaction.
5. David, a man after God's own heart, realized that his happiness consisted of being right in his life and character.
6. When David sinned, he knew he must repent to be right with God. Psalm 51 tells how he found that righteousness brings joy and happiness and also brings assurance that in the end he shall see God.

7. I hear a great deal about a happy hour in some restaurants. It seems to me it should be called the unhappy hour.

A HAPPY PERSON WILL BE **HELPFUL** (verses 7,9)

1. Karen Horney, a psychiatrist, states that many people are ailing and unhappy because they have not learned how to reach out to others.
2. When I was in Israel, I learned that the Dead Sea got its name because water flowed into it but nothing ever flowed out of it. Often we are like that. We take in blessings but don't give them out, resulting in unhappiness.
3. In Luke, Jesus told about the Good Samaritan. He condemned the action of the robbers, the priest, and the Levite and commended the action of the Good Samaritan.
4. A feeling of joy and happiness comes as we serve others cheerfully.
5. vs. 7 – We must show mercy to others in times of hurt, sickness, or when overtaken in a fault.
6. The Scripture says when we show mercy, we will obtain mercy and be happy.
7. vs. 9 – You can be helpful by being a peacemaker, not a troublemaker. Try to bring peace at home and on the job, and you will be called a happy child of God.

A HAPPY PERSON IS **HOPEFUL** (verses 10-12)

1. Jesus tells us: "There will be times when things will not be easy. You will be ridiculed and persecuted for righteous-

ness' sake. Yet be happy and hopeful, because you are My children, bound for Heaven."
2. He even said in verses 11-12 to rejoice when some say false things about you. I remind you that Jesus took ridicule. Paul was constantly in trouble. Jesus said be hopeful, for persecution brings happiness. Paul says in Philippians 4: *"Rejoice, and again I say rejoice."* Both Jesus and Paul could be saying, "When you have blues and blahs, Jesus can take these blues and blahs and turn them into oohs and aahs.
3. So let us be hopeful.
   a. Hope is one of the greatest things in the world.
   b. It is hope that keeps a weary mother going when trials of the day become difficult.
   c. It is hope that keeps the sick person looking up for the day health will return.
   d. It is hope that keeps a song in our hearts even when the world situation looks impossible.
   e. When people lose hope, they lose in life.
4. So Jesus is telling us that hope is an essential ingredient to happiness.
5. Jesus said, *"In this world you will have trials, troubles, and ups and downs, but be of good cheer, be happy and hopeful. I have overcome the world."* Remember: you are on the winning team!
6. I believe it was Browning who said that the best is yet to be.

So the blueprint for happiness, according to Jesus is:

> Humility—be humble
> Holiness—be holy
> Helpfulness—be helpful
> Hopefulness—be hopeful

This chorus sums it all up:

> *Happiness is to know the Savior,*
> *Living a life within His favor,*
> *Having a change in my behavior;*
> *Happiness is the Lord.*

Huz and Buz
Genesis 22:15-21

INTRODUCTION

I apologize to Huz and Buz right now. They had no idea they would be in a sermon over 4000 years from the time of their birth. If I do them an injustice, I shall apologize when I meet them in Heaven. If they did not get to Heaven, I will let someone else apologize for me.

Everything about Huz and Buz could be written on a postage stamp. Everything they did, according to the Bible, can be put in a few words:

- They lived – they raised their families – they died. The last two have to be assumed.
- Traces can be found of them in other books, so they must have had families.
- They died, for that is the way of all flesh.
- Their ancestry was good. They were sons of Abraham's brother Nahor.
- I believe Huz and Buz were proud of Uncle Abraham. God used him. God blessed him. God had chosen him.
- What were their accomplishments? None.
- I know there are many in the Bible who did not do great things, but they did not have the misfortune to be named Huz and Buz.

The great masses of people are like Huz and Buz. They have no unusual faith, no revivals kindled, no daring deeds done, no good influence, no lives touched, no character molded, no reformation started, no spiritual victories, no altars built, nothing done for the good of others or the glory of God. So many people live and die and are forgotten and never missed. Surely God does not mean for this to be the story of my life, of your life, of the lives of others. God wants us to live victorious lives, purposeful lives.

Now, with this as a background, I make three suggestions for us and others.

STRIVE WITH GOD'S HELP TO MAKE YOUR LIFE A **TORCH** TO SHINE TO OTHERS

Jesus said. *"Let your light so shine"* (Matthew 5:16). Jesus said of John the Baptist, *"He was a bright and shining light"* (John 5:35). Paul says, *"Now that you know the Light of the World, walk as children of light"* (Philippians 2:15).

The world is in **darkness**. We need to shine as lights. The darkness is not dispelled by art, education, or culture. The light is Christ.

The world is in **danger**. We must shine. World systems are doomed. Every soul outside of Christ is doomed. It is important that we shine.

The world is in **doubt**. Satan is the author of doubt. We must shine.

Light dispels **darkness**, **danger**, and **doubt**.

MAKE YOUR LIFE A **TESTIMONY** TO THE SAVING GRACE OF THE LORD JESUS CHRIST

Paul was a trophy of God's grace. He said, *"I am what I am by the grace of God."* He became a marvelous, glorious testimony of grace.

Peter and John in Acts 3 testified about their

Lord.

Your life should be a testimony at home, at work, and in associations with others. A good sign that you are a trophy of God's grace is your willingness to give your testimony to others. Every saved soul is a trophy of God's grace.

MAKE YOUR LIFE A **TRIUMPH** FOR GOD'S GLORY

For God's glory, **live victoriously**. God wants you to. Christ's death made it possible. The Holy Spirit is here to help. The Bible shows the way.

For God's glory, **die victoriously**. Stephen did. Paul did. I have seen some glorious deaths.

Also, **enter God's presence victoriously**. We don't know about Huz and Buz, but we can know about ourselves. For us, to be absent from the body is to be present with the Lord.

SUMMARY

Make your life a *torch* to shine to others.

Make your life a *testimony* to God's grace.

Make your life a *triumph* for God's glory.

Why Be Good?
Luke 15:25-30

INTRODUCTION

The story of the prodigal son represents God's reception of sinners. The story of the elder brother represents the attitude of self-righteous Pharisees.

The urge to be bad is within us all, and if it doesn't break out in one form it will break out in another. Even the apostle Paul, saint that he was, could say, *"When I would do good, evil is present within me."*

We are fighting evil on every side. Jesus fought evil on every side, though He had no evil within. Our Lord knows the difficulty of living right in a world gone wrong. It is not an easy task, but it is not an impossible task.

The forces of evil surround us, and we are no match for them. Ephesians 6:12 – *We wrestle against evil powers.* There is a tendency to let go, and this spirit is abroad now more than ever before.

The elder son in this story had a right to complain, "Why be good?" His father treated the prodigal son as a hero after he broke his father's heart, spent all his money, and dragged the family name down. The elder son had been faithful to his dad. He had milked cows, raised crops, never given Dad trouble. The elder son had the wrong spirit, a bad attitude (why should I be good?).

God is calling Christians to walk in paths of righteousness for His name sake. I want to suggest three reasons why we ought to be good.

BE GOOD BECAUSE YOU ARE **LOOKING IN**

You will always know yourself as no one else knows you. You may do things that no one else will discover, but you cannot run from yourself. Be sure your sins will find you out.

1. Your sins, not other people, will find you out.
2. Your conscience and subconscious does not let you get away with it.
3. Your sins will write their signature on your blood pressure and nervous system, rob you of sleep, and rob you of peace. Your life will become a walking nightmare. (Judas betrayed Christ, then his life was a nightmare.)

The poet says it rightly:

I have to live with myself, and so
I want to be fit for myself, to know;
I want to be able as the days go by,
Always to look myself straight in the eye;
I don't want to stand with the setting sun
And hate myself for the things I've done;

Be good, for you must live with yourself.

BE GOOD BECAUSE OTHERS ARE **LOOKING ON**

Not only are you responsible for yourself, but the destiny of others depends on your conduct and character. We are in a community; we influence friends, loved ones, and children. The old adage "It's my business what I do" is not actually true. We are interrelated.

Paul said, *"No person lives to himself and no man dies to himself."* Immanuel Kant, philosopher, said, "Live so that if everyone imitated you it would bring the greatest good. Illustration: Paul (1 Corinthians 8:13): *"If eating meat offends anyone, I will eat no meat."*

Be good; don't cause people to do wrong.

May God help us to live right because of others! You are the salt—you are light.

BE GOOD BECAUSE GOD IS **LOOKING DOWN**

If everyone knew you as God knows you, would your friends respect you? You may hide many things from others. You may hide some things from yourself. He knows every thought, every sin, every evil. He knows every weak moment, every iniquity, every hidden sin.

David said: *"If I take the wings of the morning and fly to the uttermost parts of the Earth, behold God is there."*

1. Some young people ask this question today—Why be good? Popular young people are the ones who lower moral bars. The girls who lower the bars get all the telephone calls.

2. Business people often feel the same way. If they play the game according to the rules, it seems to have no glamor. The best way to make money and get ahead is to cheat and cut corners.

3. Partners in marriage are often perplexed with the same problem: "Why be good? Other couples are unfaithful to one another and lie to one another, and they seem to get along and are happy."

What people don't seem to realize is that the game of life is a long one. And what seems to be getting away with sin is simply the patience of God at work, trying to retrieve the erring soul.

Ecclesiastes 8:11 – *Because judgment upon an evil work is not expected speedily, the hearts of people set in them to do evil.* When judgment doesn't come, the person thinks he is getting away with sin... the mills of God grind slowly. Be not deceived. God is looking down but not to snoop and pounce in judgment on you. His abiding vigil is concerned with our spiritual growth.

Why be good? Because you are looking in. Because others are looking on. Because God is looking down.

I remind you we cannot be good in our own strength:

If you confess with your mouth the Lord Jesus Christ and believe in your heart that God has raised Him from the dead, you will be saved (Romans 10:9-10).

Goodness does not begin by quitting sin, but by allowing Christ to forgive sin (Colossians 1:14 and 1 John 1:9). The beginning of goodness is salvation. Goodness must become rooted in the righteousness of Christ.

The Genius of Patience
James 1:2-4

INTRODUCTION

The New Revised Version translates verse 4 this way: *And let patience have its full effect, so that you may be mature, lacking in nothing.*

The attribute of patience is always best. However, with individuals like you and me, our patience wears thin with people and situations. How? Let me mention a few:

1. Waiting too long at a checkout place in a grocery store or department store

2. A long wait at a fast food restaurant

3. Waiting 30 or 45 minutes for food at a restaurant

4. Driving behind a slow driver on the highway

5. Not too long ago, I heard a lady say, "I am so impatient with my children. Pray for me."

6. Someone who is never ready or always late for a meeting

William Carey, father of our modern mission movement, said, "I can plod. That is my only genius. I can persevere in any definite pursuit. I owe everything to patience and endurance."

English sculptor Charles Jagger aspired to create a statue of Jesus that would move people to repentance and adoration when they viewed it. He worked harder and harder. He was ready to give up when, Jagger says, Jesus appeared at the door, saying, "Try it again." Today the statue stands at Kelham, England, a benediction to all who see it.

Noah Webster's dictionary was 36 years in the making. Abraham Lincoln suffered eight political defeats and business failures before he was elected President of the United States. Thomas Edison, discoverer of the electric light bulb, testified, "Did it come easy? I made trial after trial again and again until it came out right." Patience spelled success for these men. It can for others.

I want to say four things about patience.

PATIENCE IS AN ATTRIBUTE OF GOD

Have you thought of how patient God is? He was a long time creating the world (Genesis 2:2). Since the fall of man (Genesis 3:24), He has been working constantly to bring the human race back to Himself. For thousands and thousands of years, He has moved ceaselessly toward the fulfillment of His redemptive purpose. He was patient with the children of Israel in Old Testament times (Deuteronomy 5:15). He brought them out of Egypt, but how infinitely patient He was with them! How longsuffering He was and how forbearing in the face of their continued backsliding! It took forty years of wandering in the wilderness.

But God is just as patient with our world today. Martin Luther once said, "If I were God, and the world had treated me as it treated Him, I would kick the wretched world into pieces." Let me remind you how patient God is with you and me:

    a. We have sinned.
    b. We have failed God.
    c. We have weaknesses.
    d. Many times we have been unfaithful and have disappointed God.

e. Yet how amazed we should be concerning His patience and longsuffering with us! (See Psalm 40:1-6.)
   f. How could He possibly love us so much and provide grace sufficient?

JESUS MANIFESTED THE PATIENCE OF GOD
   1. He dealt with His erring, faltering disciples with loving patience and persistence.
   2. He accepted the abuse heaped on Him by His enemies with serenity and grace.
   3. He suffered indignities and unspeakable cruelties with calm acceptance and composure. Indeed, He was divinely patient in every situation with all people.

   Edward Denny wrote:

   *What grace, O Lord, and beauty shone
   around Thy steps below!
   What patient love was seen in all
   Thy life and death of woe!*

   4. And we are to be like Jesus. When we become impatient, we are out of harmony with Him. We must share His longsuffering, His gentleness and persevering love.
   5. We must be patient with others, remembering how patient God is with us and with them.
   6. We must be patient in the presence of failures and frustration, knowing that perseverance wins.
   7. We must be patient in our trials and tribulations, realizing that everything is under God's control and will be fashioned

into a pattern of good (Hebrews 12:1; James 1:4). The patience of Jesus must be reflected in our lives.

WE MUST BE PATIENT IN PRAYER

1. Look at Luke 18:1 – *Then Jesus told His disciples a parable to show them that they should pray and not give up.* Many times our prayers fall short because we do not persevere. We must keep on praying until the answer comes. Just keep on praying.

2. For sixty years the great man George Muller prayed daily for the salvation of two men. One converted before he died and the other afterwards. Likewise, my brother Chuck relates a story about ten men whom a cancer patient had on his prayer list. All ten men have committed to Christ. I read about a woman who prayed for her husband fifteen years before he was saved.

3. Many times prayer is required over a long period, not because God is unwilling to answer, but because barriers to the reception of His answer must be cleared away.

4. *Pray without ceasing* – 1 Thessalonians 5:17.

WE MUST BE PATIENT IN SERVICE

1. Paul says, *"Let us not be weary in well-doing, for in due season we shall reap, if we faint not"* (Galatians 6:9).

2. How prone we are to give up when things don't go right and we don't see the fruit of our labor! This is being shortsighted.

3. Some years ago a Sunday School teacher invited a group of underprivileged boys to come to his house, and he fitted them with new clothes to wear to Sunday School. One of the boys was absent the first week, present the second week, then he soiled his suit. But he was given another a few weeks later and eventually came regularly. That boy became a Christian, a teacher, and a minister.
4. Jesus said (Luke 8:15) that you know you will have a good harvest to lay at His feet someday if you will develop one virtue: the attribute of patient and faithful service.
5. 1 Timothy 6:11 – *O man of God (and woman of God), follow after patience!*

    Someone has written, "Teach us Thy patience, forgive our quick tempers, help us to think before being impatient."

The Bible's Greatest Promise (and my favorite verse of Scripture)
Philippians 4:19

¹⁹*And my God will supply all your needs according to His riches in glory in Christ Jesus.*

INTRODUCTION

Some years ago I bought a box of Bible verses that were labeled *God's Promises from the Scripture*. As I looked through them, the one that caught my attention was Philippians 4:19. Why this one, when there were other great promises?

1. John 3:16—the promise of salvation
2. John 10:27-28—the promise of eternal life
3. Philippians 4:6-7—the promise of God's provision
4. Romans 8:28—the promise of suffering's triumph

All of these and many more are precious promises from God. However, the one that stands out to me is found in Philippians 4:19.

THAT PROMISE IS GREAT TO ME BECAUSE IT IS A **PERSONAL** PROMISE

1. It begins with the words, *"My God..."* Not any God, or a god, but my God. Paul is not referring to gods of the Greeks, Romans, Assyrians, Babylonians, or Egyptians, not the Islamic god or the Buddhist god.
2. When Paul said, *"My God..."* he was being very specific and personal. Paul's God was

the covenant God who had revealed Himself to men in the person of Jesus Christ. This God is a great God, a gracious, loving, powerful, and effective God.

    a. The God of Philippians 4:19 is the God of Abraham. He was the God who called Abraham and sent him into a new land and promised him that he would be blessed and would be a blessing to his people.

    b. The God of Philippians 4:19 is the God who spoke to David the shepherd and made him King of Israel.

    c. The God of Philippians 4:19 is the God who called Jeremiah, even before he was born, to be a prophet.

    d. The God of Philippians 4:19 is the God who spoke to Isaiah, giving him a personal call. He responded by saying, *"Here I am. Send me."*

    e. The God of Philippians 4:19 is the God who spoke to Peter and John. He made them *fishers of men.*

    f. The God of Philippians 4:19 is the God who raised His only begotten Son out of cold death to a resurrected power and life.

That is what a personal God can do for anyone who trusts in Jesus.

IT IS THE GREATEST PROMISE BECAUSE IT'S SO VERY **POSITIVE**

    1. God says, *"I will supply."* The word *supply* literally means *fill up* or *fill to the fullest.*

2. The words *will supply* are God's divine affirmative, the everlasting *yes.* Whatever your need, He will supply (not your wants but your needs).
3. This is the Bible's greatest promise because we are promised God's providential love and care.
4. We are a bundle of needs from the cradle to the grave.
5. A word of caution about needs: we must leave the interpretation of needs in higher hands than our own.
6. We must be careful about transforming our wants into needs.
7. The spiritual effect can be bad when our wants and our whims are not met, and we begin to wonder if we can count on God.
8. Alexander MacLaren said, "The truth of the matter is that whatever we do not obtain, we do not require or need."
9. However, I believe the Lord delights to grant what we really need. What are some of those needs?

   a. You have need of forgiveness. He has promised in 1 John 1:8-9, *"If we say that we have no sin, we deceive ourselves and the truth is not in us. If we confess our sins, He is faithful and just to forgive us our sins and to cleanse us from all unrighteousness."*

   b. Are you out of fellowship with God? Augustine said that "God has made us for Himself, and our hearts are restless until they find their rest in Him."

Psalm 42:1 – *My soul pants for You, O God.*

Psalm 27:1 – *The Lord is my light and my salvation. Whom shall I fear? The Lord is the strength of my life. Of whom shall I be afraid?*

  c. Are you afraid? Psalm 56:3 – *What time I am afraid I will trust in Thee.*

  d. Have you ever had the need of overcoming temptation? 1 Corinthians 10:13 – *No temptation has overtaken you except what is common to man. God is faithful, and He will not allow you to be tempted beyond what you are able, but will with the temptation also provide a way of escape, so that you are able to bear it.* When you are tempted, God will help you escape. As one wise man put it, "When I hear the Devil knocking on my door, realizing that he wants to tempt me, I send Jesus to answer the door."

  e. Are you having a personal need or trial that is testing your faith? Listen again to the Psalmist: *"My help comes from the Lord."*

PHILIPPIANS 4:19 IS THE GREATEST PROMISE BECAUSE IT'S FILLED WITH **PLENTY**

1. The Scripture says, *"...according to the riches of His glory..."* This phrase opens up the treasures of divine life and love from God, the Owner of all.

  a. Romans 2:4 talks about the riches of God's goodness.

b. Romans 11:33 talks about the riches of His wisdom.

c. Ephesians 1:7 talks about the riches of His grace.

d. Ephesians 3:16 talks about the riches of His glory.

PHILIPPIANS 4:19 IS THE GREATEST PROMISE BECAUSE OF THE LIVING **PRESENCE** OF THE ONE WHO GUARANTEES OUR NEED WILL BE MET

1. This is seen in the words *"in Christ Jesus."*
2. *"Riches in glory"* seems high, beyond our reach.
3. But when Paul added *"...in Christ Jesus,"* he brings them down amongst us. If we are in Him, we are always right beside our treasures and only have to put out our hands and receive.
4. All that we need is ours *"in Christ"*.
5. He is the living Presence to meet our needs. He is adequate. He says, *"I am with you."*
6. Paul sums it up when he says that God gives us power for the things we do and for our needs to be met. He gives us plenty.

CLOSING

I believe this verse was penned in order that we might just remember *Jesus*, for all God's promises are in Him.

The Life of Christ

Jesus' Birth and the Angels
Luke 2:9-14

INTRODUCTION

The study of angelology is interesting and fascinating. Theologians differ as to the function of angels. But in general angels are <u>messengers</u>, ministers for God. They were created by the Infinite One to aid in carrying out His divine purpose—the purpose of revealing Himself to mankind. Thus, wherever and whenever an angel of the Lord or angels are mentioned in the Old Testament or New Testament, they perform a work—they have a function—and that function is to make known God to man and help bring man to God.

Five times during the life and ministry of Jesus the Savior, the evangelists picture the angelic messengers ministering for Him and unto Him.

1. At His birth
2. After His temptation
3. In His agony at Gethsemane
4. At His resurrection
5. At His ascension

Today, we are primarily interested in the birth of Jesus and what part the angels played in this historic event. The cradle of Bethlehem commands our attention at this season. Briefly let your imagination look back over 1900 years ago.

    1. See Joseph and Mary making their way to Bethlehem.

2. Reaching this historic city.
3. Joseph looking for lodging.
4. The inn is crowded.
5. Tired and weary, no place could be found.
6. Their refuge became a cave in the limestone rock, used as a stable for horses and a den for cattle.
7. Here the horses' manger becomes a cradle for the King of Kings—the Savior was born.

There were attendants to the birth of Jesus:

1. The angels were there.
2. The shepherds were nearby.
3. The wise men came later.

But let us notice the prominent part the angels had in the events that surrounded the birth of Jesus.

THE ANGELS' **AUDIENCE**

1. The importance of the birth in Bethlehem, unrecognized by man, is realized by angels.
2. On that starlit night, the heavenly host could not be silent about such a blessed event. They must tell the good news!
3. Whom should they tell? Where will the ones be found who shall receive the message?
    a. The inn is full of sleepers and revelers. They are not in any condition to hear the message of peace and joy.
    b. Not the scribes and Pharisees at Jerusalem.

c. But outside Bethlehem in the field are shepherds—humble men, despised men—yet men who were kind to their flock.
   d. These men became the recipients of the angels' message. Awake and watchful, they hear the angelic message.
   e. For whom is God's message today? Not the proud but the sinner. He came to call sinners to repentance.

THE ANGELS' **ANNOUNCEMENT**

1. What was the message? The greatest, grandest, most glorious announcement that the world has ever heard came from an angel. Listen to this message:

Behold! I bring you good tidings of great joy which shall be to all the people. Today in the city of David a Savior has been born, Christ the Lord! This will be a sign for you: you will find a babe wrapped in swaddling clothes and lying in a manger.

2. Notice this about the message:
   a. the substance (verse 11): born this day a Savior
   b. the character (verse 10): good tidings of great joy
   c. the sign (verse 12): a baby wrapped in swaddling clothes

3. What an announcement! What a message! God became flesh to become my personal Savior. He is mine. What about you?

THE ANGELS' **ADORATION**

I have listened to a symphonic orchestra playing the classics, marveled at the voice of George Beverly Shea, and heard a choir sing Handel's *Messiah,* but no music could ever compare to the beauty, simplicity, praise, and melodious words of that angelic choir.

The angels had arranged for a service of praise. They had something to sing about. They had Someone to praise. They were praising God for His gift—Jesus in the manger of Bethlehem.

Glory to God in the highest,
And on earth peace and goodwill to men!

The Greatest Battle Ever Fought
Matthew 4:1-11

INTRODUCTION

Many great battles have decided the future course of the human race:

1) In A.D. 732 Charles Martel and his armed forces turned back the Islamic army at Tours, France and prevented Islam from sweeping Western Europe.
2) Another kind of battle was fought at Worms, Germany in 1521, when Martin Luther stood before King Charles V and the princes of Germany and took his stand on the rock of Scripture.
3) But the greatest battle in the history of the universe took place in a desert in Judea where Jesus Christ, the Son of God, met Satan, whom the Bible calls the Devil.

The Bible says that Satan is Lucifer, the *son of the morning*. He is the *prince of the powers of the air*. He is the *god of this age*, the *tempter*, the *adversary* of mankind. And at the time of his encounter with Jesus, he was in the prime of his condition. He had been training a long time, getting ready to fight. Satan had already defeated Adam and Eve in the Garden of Eden and was ready for another fight.

The Bible tells us that when the battle took place, Jesus was hungry. He had fasted for forty days and nights. He was so weak He could hardly stand to His feet. He had the wild beasts for His companions and a stone for His pillow. When He faced Satan in the desert wilderness, it was in all the weakness of human flesh.

Today, I want you to sit in the stands of the arena and watch that battle. The demons in Hell prepare to watch. The angels in Heaven stand by looking on. If Satan wins, Hell will be our fate and Satan will be enthroned as ruler of the universe.

THE FIRST ROUND IN THE BATTLE

"If you are the Son of God, command these stones to become loaves of bread."

Satan's appeal was to Jesus' hunger. Jesus could have done this miracle, but He looked at Satan and referred to Deuteronomy 8:3, saying, *"Yes, a man has to live by bread but not by bread alone, not by things but by the Word of God."*

Jesus uses the sword of His Word. The round ends. Hell puts on mourning. Heaven rejoices.

Some try to escape temptation in the wrong way. The best escape is the Word of God.

ROUND TWO BEGINS

Satan appeals to pride. He takes Jesus this time to the pinnacle of the Temple of Jerusalem, hundreds of feet above the ground.

"If you are the Son of God, throw yourself down; for it is written, 'He will give His angels charge of You, and on their hands they will bear You up, lest You strike Your foot against a stone.'"

The Devil knows more Scripture than the average Christian does. He misquotes it and takes it out of context. This is how people today are fooled by cults.

Satan said, "Jump off this pinnacle, and everybody will see the angels catching You in midair. They will believe You are the Son of God, and You won't have to go the cross."

Satan was trying to get Jesus to take a shortcut to glory. Jesus again pointed the Sword of the Spirit, the Word of God, at Satan and quoted Scripture: *"It is written, 'You shall not tempt the Lord your God.'"*

Notice that Satan did not argue with Him. Satan cannot argue with Scripture. The reason so many fall to the temptations of Satan is that they don't use the Bible. We don't know it enough, and we don't quote it. Meanwhile, the temptation gets appealing. But if we quote Scripture to Satan, he backs off (only to try again later).

The bell rings, ending the second round. Again Hell puts on mourning while angels rejoice. Satan is wounded. He's down but not out. He has another plan.

ROUND THREE

This time Satan uses his most severe punch: ambition. He takes Christ to the crest of a high mountain and says to Him, "Jesus, You see below You all the kingdoms of the world—Babylon, Crete, Persia, Rome, Greece, Hollywood, Times Square. **If you bow down and worship me, I'll give You the whole thing, and it will be Yours forever.**"

Jesus never disputed Satan's ability to give the world to Him. Satan is the prince of this world. He controls it by the permissive will of God. He has political power and economic power.

That is the way Satan works. "I will give you pleasure, money, and prestige if you follow me and worship me."

So once again Jesus goes back to the Word of God. Satan stands there while all the universe holds its breath, for this is the final round, the last attempt. Satan has used his last trick. What will Jesus do? He speaks: *"It is written, 'You shall worship the Lord your God, and Him only shall you serve.'"*

He hurls this text at Satan, and Satan goes down. The Referee of the universe says, "One, two... ten – Satan is out!"

CLOSING

Today, Satan is a defeated enemy conquered by the love of Jesus Christ for us. The demons of Hell are mourning. Jesus has been crowned as victor. The morning stars sing together. Angels and archangels rejoice. God has smiled approval upon His Son. The Enemy has been defeated, the battle won.

Jesus Christ is the Commander-in-Chief of the forces of God. He is the Captain of our salvation, and He is leading us to a glorious and splendid victory. One day the nations of the world will bow their knees to Christ and confess Him with their mouths as Lord and Master and King, and Satan will spend eternity in the lake of fire.

Jesus was alone when the temptation came to Him. Satan will do the same to you. But remember Paul's words (1 Corinthians 10:13): *God is faithful when you are tempted to make a way of escape.*

Jesus was weak. When you are at your weakest moment, Satan will attack. Jesus did not yield to the tempter. He used the Sword of the Spirit to drive the Devil back. Satan can be overcome. He can be forced to flee. How did Christ gain the victory?

1) By obedience to the will of God
2) By surrender to the Holy Spirit
3) By spending much time in prayer
4) By knowing the Scripture

Consider the words of this hymn:

Yield not to temptation, for yielding is sin;
Each vict'ry will help you some other to win.
Fight manfully onward, dark passions subdue;
Look ever to Jesus. He'll carry you through.

His First Message
Mark 1:14-22

INTRODUCTION

It was a dramatic moment in the ministry of Jesus when He delivered His first message. Knowing that His ministry would last only three years, Jesus did not want to waste a single word. He knew full well what was in the heart of man. What would He say?

The time is fulfilled;
the Kingdom of God is at hand.
Repent and believe the gospel.

He was fresh from the rigors of temptation and fresh from the waters of baptism. These words, recorded in Mark 1:15, constitute His first message preached. He declared in this brief message the major thrust of His ministry. No doubt He repeated this message again and again.

THE SERMON WAS SPIRITUAL IN ITS CONTENT

1. Surprisingly, Jesus didn't touch on the vital social issues of the day.
2. The people were facing any number of problems:
    a. Taxation was a problem. People were taxed 40% to 70%. Jesus was silent.
    b. Many of them were slaves. Jesus did not touch on slavery.
    c. Nowhere in the sermon did He speak about social issues.
3. He spoke to the need for spiritual renewal in the heart of man.

      a. Jesus believed with all His heart that man was his own worst enemy.
      b. The problem was not the environment or the institutions of society.
      c. Man's heart must be right with God.
4. Illustration: In one western serial, the cowboys did not realize that they were shooting in the wrong direction. The bad guy was somewhere else. We, too, are shooting in the wrong direction if we don't realize that the heart of man is the target. Man's chief need is being right with God.
5. Earnest Campbell said, "If a man's chief need were education, there would be a school at the heart of history. If man's chief need were self-analysis, there would be a psychiatrist's couch. If scientific prowess, there would be a scientific laboratory at the heart of history. But there is a cross at the heart of history, because man's great fundamental need is that he might be redeemed by the saving grace of God."

JESUS' FIRST MESSAGE RANG WITH URGENCY

Man says, "Let me be first." Jesus said, *"Seek first the kingdom of God."* He comes to teenagers. He comes to college students. He comes to young couples after marriage. He comes to us when children are given to us. He comes to us when we're older.

How often our hearts are hard and cold and we cannot come! Jesus wept over Jerusalem: *"How often would I have gathered Thy children together, even as a hen gathereth her chickens under her wings, and ye would not."* The reluctance is never on God's side. It's always on our side.

There were four points in Jesus' first sermon. It is made up of two assertions (*the time is fulfilled; the Kingdom of God is at hand*) and two imperatives (*repent* and *believe*). Today, consider these imperatives.

REPENT!

1. Did you ever stop to think that God never says, "Please"? There's no coaxing in this message of Jesus.
2. Jesus' sermon was addressed to those who thought they had the inside track with God. It seems almost a pity to waste a sermon on this congregation, on those who were religious people. Many did not listen or heed.
3. We, like them, often say, "This is not for me."
4. Redemption involves the will—turning away from sins and turning to God.
5. As Christians, we must repent: repent of what we have said, repent because of our wrong actions, repent because of our wrong attitudes.

BELIEVE!

1. *Believe in the gospel*—the death, burial, and resurrection of Jesus.
2. Webster defines *belief* as confidence, trust.
3. The gospel is good news for mankind.
4. We cannot separate the gospel from Jesus Christ.
    a. Believe means to take Jesus at His word.
    b. Believe means to have faith in the good news.
    c. Believe means to exercise trust in the gospel.
    d. Believe means both head and heart belief.

5. Did they believe?
   Andrew did!
   Simon Peter did!
   Nicodemus did!
   James and John did!
   Countless men and women have.
   Have you? You can!

We Would See Jesus
John 12:20-32

INTRODUCTION

Have you ever gone to a city to visit someone important and had to go through certain channels to see the busy person? In the days of Jesus, certain Greeks came to Jerusalem to see the Master. It seems that they had to contact certain disciples before beholding the Son of God. The Scriptures indicate that they saw Philip first. He in turn talked with Andrew, and finally Andrew and Philip brought them into the presence of Jesus.

We are not told why they came. Perhaps they had heard of His miraculous works, or they had received word concerning His teaching. Many had heard news of His feeding the five thousand. Also noised abroad was His walking on top of the water. Spread everywhere was the message that He had changed many lives:

    a. The woman of Samaria
    b. The man born blind
    c. The resurrection of Lazarus

They wanted a glimpse of this unusual man.

Jesus used the visit of these Grecians to give a discourse—to set forth truths concerning Himself. With deep emotion Jesus proclaimed truths:

    1. His oneness with the Father
    2. His errand of redemption
    3. The guilt of rejecting His revelation
    4. The gift of eternal life
    5. The universality of His salvation

Just like the Greeks of old, people today want

to see Jesus:

1. It is quite evident that they cannot see Him in a physical form.

2. Yet I am convinced that people from all strata of society are desirous to see the attributes of the Master—the way and actions of Jesus—in those who have been converted, those who have been redeemed.

3. Theologians, ministers, and Bible scholars are saying, "Christianity today is losing its effectiveness because those who claim to be Christians are not exemplifying Christ in action, word, or deed." This is a serious charge against us.

PEOPLE ON THE OUTSIDE ARE LOOKING AT YOU

Today, people need to see Jesus in us. They are watching us!

Allow me to point out those who are looking at us, desiring to see Jesus in our lives. Jesus said of Christians, *"You are the salt of the earth; you are the light of the world. You are My disciples."* We must show forth Jesus. Daily our lives are being watched by those outside the Church:

    a. An unsaved husband
    b. A business friend
    c. A man on the job
    d. A friend down the street
    e. A fellow student in school

1. A famous opera singer said, "I watched the life of my Christian wife for years; she showed forth Christ—I saw Jesus in her. She led me to Christ."

2. While pastoring in Indiana in my seminary days, I talked with many outside the church. Their words staggered me – "Christians are doing the same things I do...."

3. A young doctor, approached about accepting Christ as his personal Savior, replied, "I might have become a Christian if I had not known so many people who said they were." What did he mean? Simply that many people who call themselves Christians do not show forth Christ. This is the tragedy of Christianity today.

4. If Christianity is to move forward and win the lost to the Lord, we who name the name of Christ must show forth Jesus. Those outside must see Jesus in us.

PEOPLE ON THE INSIDE ARE LOOKING AT YOU

Do they see Jesus in your life? Paul wrote, *"None of us lives to himself, and no man dies to himself."*

1. Our influence upon those who are in the Church is extremely important. Dad, mother, deacon, teacher, leader—young people in church, new Christians, and new members are looking at YOU... do they see Jesus?

2. A noted preacher tells the story of his young son doing everything he did.

3. People are likewise watching your actions.
    a. Do you show Christian love and fellowship?
    b. Are you loyal to all services of the Church?
    c. Are you, through gossip and criticism,

leaving the wrong influence?
d. Do people say about you, "He or she is a consecrated deacon, leader, or teacher"?

4. Jesus is seen in the Church when the members are united in love and dedicated in service.

GOD IS LOOKING AT YOU

Does He see Jesus in you? Does He see the Christ-like life in you?

We must remember:

1. God is all-knowing, all-seeing. The Old Testament says (Psalms)—*"For the Lord searches all hearts and understands all the imagination of the thoughts. His understanding is infinite."* 1 John 3:20—*God knows all things.* Job called God *the watcher of men.* Luke 12:2—*Nothing is hid from Him.*

2. I have known some in older days and today who thought they were getting away with sin.
   a. David
   b. Ananias and Sapphira

God knows the inner recesses of our hearts. He has telescopic eyes. Christians, children of God—knowing that people on the outside are watching you, that people on the inside are observing you, and that God is looking at you, let us say...

1. I want to live as Jesus lived.
2. I want to love as Jesus loved.
3. I want my life to honor Him in everything.

What Does Christ See in You?
Luke 14: 16-24

INTRODUCTION

What do you see in others?

Suppose you are seated in a bus station or airport and a complete stranger comes and sits down opposite you. What do you see? How do you look at this person? Do you look at the person critically? Or do you tend to look with friendly interest and think that, despite some external evidence, the person seems to be a decent individual, perhaps a potential friend?

What we see in a person is often not so much a revelation of that person as it is a revelation of ourselves. Christ saw in some of the unlikeliest people the most remarkable possibilities. When you open the Bible, you see people who don't belong there. Look at them: lepers, beggars, cripples, corrupt politicians, and thieves. As our text puts it, "the poor, the maimed, the halt, and the blind," a group of misfits, some from the very dregs of society.

Yet, strange as it may seem, many of them were friends of Jesus. He seemed perfectly at home with them. Jesus would rather be called the "friend of sinners" than any other fancy name. As Jesus mixed and mingled with these men and women, He saw in them more than we would see in them. As He invited the halt, the maimed, the poor, and the blind to the great supper. He saw in them tremendous potential.

Let us notice what Christ saw in these men and women who were classified as sinners.

CHRIST SAW THE BEST IN A PERSON

From His earthly ministry, we gather what He saw in people.

1. **Simon Peter** was an ignorant, unlearned fisherman, yet our Lord saw tremendous possibility in him. He saw a sinner saved who would become a devout follower and a great preacher.
2. In **Zacchaeus**, a man widely known for his dishonesty, Christ saw the possibility of redemption and usefulness.
3. In an outcast and immoral **woman at the well** in Sychar, Christ saw the possibility of a Christian witness. She accepted Christ as the Water of Life and went back into the city to tell others about Him.
4. In Christianity's bitterest enemy, **Paul**, Christ saw one who would become Christianity's greatest proclaimer of truth.

I believe Christ likewise sees in your city and area sinners, without Christ, as people with tremendous possibilities.

WHY CHRIST SAW THE BEST IN PEOPLE

Jesus was aware of people's sin. He didn't love or condone their sin, but He loved sinners. He saw people with an eye of compassion. He looked at them differently. He saw great possibilities in people.

Why should He love sinners?

A. He wanted to help them.
B. He wanted to redeem them.
C. He wanted to reconcile them to God.

This was His mission:
- A. He came not to call the righteous.
- B. The Son of Man came to seek and save the lost.
- C. He came to give new meaning to life.
- D. He came to change sinners from the dregs of society to the pinnacle of righteousness.
- E. He came to love the world (John 3:16).

Luther Burbank, the great American horticulturist, used to say, "Every weed is a potential flower." Jesus looked on every sinner as a potential saint. That's why He sought to change and remake them.

WHAT DOES CHRIST SEE IN YOU?

Hearing me today are Christians and perhaps a few who have not come to Christ as Savior. First, I want to ask, "What does Christ see in you as Christians?"

- A. **Saved Sinners**. I remind you what Paul wrote in Ephesians 2:8-9. *For by grace are you are saved through faith; and that not of yourselves—it is the gift of God—not of works, lest any man should boast.*
- B. **Prayer Supporters**
- C. **Church Workers**, willing to serve Christ as Sunday School teachers, on committees, as choir members, etc.
- D. **Witnesses for Jesus**
- E. **Moral Crusaders**
- F. **Tithers**
- G. **Dedicated Followers**

Find your place in service for Christ inside the church and outside the church, and you will become the person that Christ sees in you.

To those here today who may not have accepted Christ as Savior, what does Christ see in you and what does He see for you?

1. He knows your life. He knows your spiritual condition.
2. He knows that you need Him as your Savior and Lord.
3. He knows what in your life's situation keeps you from trusting Him.
4. Let me remind you that the Savior is compassionate, longsuffering, not willing that any should perish.
5. He sees you as a potential child of the King.
6. He can change your life now and make you what He wants you to be, what you ought to be.

Today, let Jesus have His way in your heart and life!

The Hands of Jesus
John 20:20

INTRODUCTION

Hands make a fascinating study. There are big hands, rough hands, smooth hands, long hands, short hands, old hands, young hands, ugly hands, beautiful hands.

There are people who tell us that the fortunes or misfortunes of life can be told by looking at our hands. Someone may say, "Give me your hand. Let me see your palm, and I will tell you whether you'll live long or whether your life will be short." Do not put too much faith in such soothsayers.

But there is a sense in which your hands reveal the real you. Hands may sometimes tell your character; certainly they give a hint as to your vocation. There are the hands of a musician, the hands of an artist, the hands of a soldier, and the hands of the laborer.

One of the world's most beautiful works of art is Albrecht Durer's *Praying Hands.* There is an interesting story about how this masterpiece came to be. One day Durer saw his friend's work-worn hands folded reverently, and he said, "I will paint your hands as they are now, folded in prayer, so the world will know my appreciation for your noble, unselfish character."

Indeed, hands do reveal character. As we think of our Lord Jesus Christ, we do not know specifically what His hands looked like. But I believe we can discover some general characteristics. In John 20:20 we read: *When He had said this, He showed them His hands.* What were the hands of Jesus like?

THE HANDS OF JESUS WERE WORKING HANDS

Our Master was a carpenter, and no doubt He used His hands busily in Joseph's carpenter shop. One scholar has pointed out that during the time that Jesus lived, Sepphoris, the capital of Galilee, was being rebuilt and that both Joseph and Jesus traveled to that city to help in its reconstruction. Jesus must have made plow-stocks which the farmers used as they worked their fields. Jesus toiled long hours, and His hands were those of a worker.

He was a hard worker as an itinerant preacher. He went about Galilee and Judea preaching and teaching. He gave Himself wholeheartedly and devotedly to His tasks.

Those of us who follow in His train must be workmen, too. Paul's words to the church in Thessalonica: *"If any man will not work, neither let him eat."* Work is a part of life. Work in church is a part of the Christian life.

The hands of Jesus were those of a workman.

THE HANDS OF JESUS WERE THE HANDS OF A STUDENT

Jesus was an ardent student of the Old Testament. The Law, the Prophets, and the Writings—He knew all well. Often He would go to the synagogue and study. He was a student of the past.

With our schools soon to open, grade school, junior high, high school, and college students should remember that the hands of Jesus were those of a student. Apply your hands, mind, and heart as you pursue your education.

It is fitting that the hands of Jesus were the hands of a student.

THE HANDS OF JESUS WERE HEALING HANDS

Jesus touched with His hands the eyes of the blind. He reached out and lifted the cripple by the hand.

In Matthew 8:1-3 a leper knelt before Him. He stretched forth His hand and touched the leper and said: *"I will; be clean."*

He also healed a man with a withered hand.

If we stretch forth our hands, we too are going to serve and minister. If we follow in Jesus' footsteps, we shall be busy using our hands and our hearts to help heal humanity's hurts.

THE HANDS OF JESUS WERE LOVING HANDS

In our imagination, we can see the boy Jesus putting His hands and arms around His mother's neck as He expressed His love.

We read in the Bible how Jesus touched with His hands the little children who were brought to Him. Oh, how He loved them!

Jesus showed love and humility by washing the disciples' feet.

You see, *love does not vaunt itself; it is not puffed up.* Love is humble. Love never asks "how much must I do?" but "how much can I do?"

The hand can either slap or caress. It can either express the desire to fight or it can express love.

One of the most famous left hands in all history was that of Jack Dempsey. Dempsey used his hands as an instrument with which to fight. Christ used His hands to love.

Paul says to greet each other with a holy kiss. He meant greet each other with a holy handshake. By the clasp of the hand we express friendship and love.

Is this not what our world needs more than anything else today? In the midst of bitterness, hatred, misunderstanding, and strife, we need the loving hand that will reach across barriers and express understanding. Truly, love is the greatest!

THE HANDS OF JESUS WERE CREATIVE HANDS

John 1:3 – *All things were made by Him, and without Him was not anything made that was made.*

He created the world.

He created you.

He created Moses and all the prophets.

He created Mary, the mother of Jesus.

He created a way of salvation for you.

He created your family, a home on earth.

He created a home in Heaven for you.

He can create a clean heart in you today.

Yes, His hands have always been creating hands, and today they reach out to you. They are ready to make something of your life today. Then you, like Him, can use your hands to work for God, to study for Him, and to love in His name.

When Impossible Things Become Possible
Luke 18:27

INTRODUCTION

It is important to notice that it was the Lord Jesus who spoke about the possibility of impossible things becoming possible. The entire Bible is a commentary on these words, and the truth has been abundantly demonstrated through the centuries. Best of all, it is being demonstrated today. We must remember that God is not only all-wise and all-loving but is also all-powerful, and it is because of this that *"the things which are impossible with men are possible with God."*

What are the things which God can do? Some of them are mentioned in Luke 18.

IT IS POSSIBLE FOR GOD TO ANSWER THE PERSISTENT PRAYER.

If an unjust judge will respond favorably to a persistent petitioner (vs. 1-8), might not we count on God to answer His own people who pray earnestly? This widow prevailed because of her importunity.

IT IS POSSIBLE FOR GOD TO SAVE THE VERY WORST SINNER.

We see this in the verses (9-14) concerning the Pharisee and the publican. The Pharisee reported to God how satisfied he was with himself. He was dignified, strutting like a peacock. The tax collector wouldn't look up but smote his chest, praying, *"God be merciful to me, a sinner."* He was justified. However sinful a person may be, God can save all.

IT IS POSSIBLE FOR GOD TO MAKE HIMSELF KNOWN TO LITTLE CHILDREN.

Look at Luke 18:15-17. Some people do not believe in child evangelism and conversion. But if a child is old enough to know right from wrong, he is old enough to be saved from the penalty of his wrongdoing. Jesus, the only begotten Son of God, welcomed the children to come to Him.

IT IS POSSIBLE FOR GOD TO DELIVER US FROM THE ALLUREMENTS OF THE WORLD.

Note Luke 18: 18-27. It is very hard for a rich man to be saved, but it is not impossible. How hard is it? The Needle's Eye was the very small gate or archway into the city. It was difficult for the tall and laden camel to go through this archway, but it was not impossible. In the same way, it is possible for rich people to come to God if they renounce their riches. In other words, they are to take their hands off them and to reckon that they don't belong to them at all but to the Lord. I have seen God deliver individuals from the allurements of the world.

IT IS POSSIBLE FOR GOD TO COMPENSATE ANY SACRIFICE WE MAY BE CALLED UPON TO MAKE.

See Luke 18:28-30. Think of missionaries who have made great sacrifices. They have left their home, a good salary, and even their children in order to proclaim the gospel. The world says these people are mad, out of their minds.

Remember: no man really gives up anything for Christ. He receives so much from Christ now and hereafter. This does not mean that following Christ is like striking a bargain that assures greater returns. But God has the power, if He chooses, to compensate a man for any sacrifice he makes.

IT IS POSSIBLE FOR GOD TO FULFILL EVERY PROMISE HE HAS MADE.

This is brought out in verses 31-34. Could Jesus' prediction be fulfilled? Yes! It came to pass. He keeps all promises.

IT IS POSSIBLE FOR GOD TO PERFORM A GREAT MIRACLE.

Let's notice verses 35-43. A man completely blind was made to see—impossible with man but possible with God. We all face trying situations, problems so great that we feel they cannot be solved. Humanly speaking, there does not seem to be a way out. But bring God into the situation and relay your situation to the Lord. He performs miracles. The blind beggar kept on asking for mercy. Don't give up!

Someone has written:

Got any rivers that are uncrossable,
Any mountains you can't tunnel through?
God specializes in things impossible.
He does things others can't do.

In summary:

1. It is possible for God to answer prayer.
2. It is possible for God to save the worst sinner.

3. It is possible for God to save children.
4. It is possible for God to deliver us from world possessions and allurements.
5. It is possible for God to bless us now and in eternity for great sacrifices.
6. It is possible for God to fulfill every promise.
7. It is possible for God to perform miracles.

Jesus Weeping on Palm Sunday
Luke 19:41 – John 11:35

INTRODUCTION

There is no more important mountain related to both past and future events in human history than the Mount of Olives in Jerusalem. It was there on the eastern slope that our Lord made His triumphant entry into Jerusalem over palm branches a few days before His own crucifixion. It was on this mountain that Scripture records the weeping of Christ. On the eastern slope of this mountain, overlooking the city of Jerusalem, Jesus wept over our sorrows. He wept over our sins.

Many believe that Palm Sunday is about a big celebration. People were shouting hosannas and waving their palm branches as Jesus rode a donkey into the city. However, I believe Palm Sunday is about weeping, tears; it is about crying.

Some have said that we have two generations in the western world who seemingly have lost their tears. Our culture has taught us that it's inappropriate to cry. We often tell our sons, "Be a man. Don't cry!" One of the major problems facing our culture is that we have lost our tears.

Eye doctors tell us that crying may be a chemical release from emotional stress. It relieves stress. This is why we often feel better after crying.

As the Lord Jesus stood at the tomb of Lazarus, He was saying it is alright to cry. God gives us tears. (No other animal species cries. We do.) Tears are a gift of God. Jesus is telling us on this Palm Sunday that it is okay to cry. He did Himself. This is why King David said that *"weeping may endure for a night, but joy comes in the morning."*

There are two places in Scripture that record Him weeping, both on the Mount of Olives. Once, on the western slope, He wept over our sorrow. He is touched by our broken heart. The other occasion, on the eastern slope, He wept over our sin. He is troubled by our blinded eyes. His tears speak volumes to us today. He still grieves even today.

TODAY IS PALM SUNDAY, AND HE CONTINUES TO GRIEVE OVER OUR **SORROW**.

He is touched by our broken hearts. Read John 11:33-35. The event was the funeral in Bethany of His dear friend Lazarus.

Note that when the Lord wept, He wept when He saw Mary crying. Mary's heart was broken. Her brother was dead, and Jesus was too late. She had no hope. She was hurting. When our Lord arrived on the scene, He saw her weeping. John uses an interesting word in the New Testament Greek language to describe Mary weeping. The word means *deep sobs, wails.*

Our Lord had come from a place where there is no sin, no sorrow, no tears, no tombs, no hurts. He walks upon the scene and sees her crying with deep and loud sobs. When our Lord saw Mary crying, He groaned in His spirit and was troubled.

Many tears and much heartbreak are caused by sin and death. Even today they still bring pain.

Mary wept and Jesus wept. The tense of the word *wept* tells us He could not hold it in.

It's Palm Sunday, and Jesus is grieving over our sorrows because He is touched by our broken hearts. Jesus is a man of sorrows, acquainted with grief.

What about the shedding of tears? Paul did. Acts 20:19 – *"I serve the Lord with humility and tears."* 2 Corinthians 2:4 – *"With much anguish and affliction of heart I wrote to you with many tears."* In Ecclesiastes 3:4 Solomon reminds us there is a time for tears.

If you need God's attention, try tears. Tears speak louder than words. Tears have a language all their own and need no interpreter. All of us who have raised children know this to be true. Any of us who have held our husbands or wives in a time of tears knows this is true. Tears move the heart of God.

Yes, it's Palm Sunday, and Jesus is grieved over our sorrows. He is touched by our broken hearts. To the government you may be only a number, a social security number, but you're somebody to God. The same Lord Jesus who saw Mary's tears and wept with her stands by your side today. He is saying to us across the centuries, "It is okay to cry." He is touched by our broken hearts.

TODAY IS PALM SUNDAY, AND JESUS IS STILL GRIEVING OVER OUR **SIN**.

Read Luke 19:41. A few days after the experience in Bethany, now on the eastern slope of the Mount of Olives, Jesus finds Himself on the back of a donkey making a triumphant entry into the city of Jerusalem. The scene is filled with excitement. A cheering crowd is waving palm branches.

However, our Lord knew that within five days their cheers would turn to jeers. Luke said, *"Now as He drew near Jerusalem, He saw the city and wept over it."* They were adoring Him, but He was weeping. Listen to what He said through His tears:

If you had known in this day, even you, the things that make for peace! But now they have been hidden from your eyes. For the days will come upon you when your enemies will throw up a barricade against you, and surround you and hem you in on every side, and they will level you to the ground and your children within you, and they will not leave in you one stone upon another, because you did not recognize the time of your visitation.

Less than a week after they crowned Him as king, they were ready to crucify Him. So our Lord sat on the Mount of Olives and wept. The Greek word for this weeping means deep sobs. He broke down and cried with deep sobs that could be heard by those nearby.

Yes, it is Palm Sunday, and Jesus is grieving over our sins. He is troubled by our rejection, our blindness. I remind you what Jesus said on one occasion, "*How often I wanted to gather My children together, as a hen gathers her chickens under her wing, but you were not willing!*"

The Church today does not seem to be grieving over the sins of people. We are blinded to what is taking place. We are watching the decay that is taking place all over. Consider our schools. Yesterday's problems were chewing gum, running, and littering. Today we see shootings, drugs, robberies, and murder. This is American in the 21st century, and Jesus is grieving.

How about us? Today's Church may have lost her tears. So on this Palm Sunday let us examine ourselves and make sure, in the midst of the celebration of His entrance into the city, that we have a deep concern about our personal sin and blindness. Jesus did, and we must.

CLOSING

General William Booth, the founder of the Salvation Army, once sent a two-word telegram to some discouraged workers: TRY TEARS. When sorrow and hurt overwhelm you, when sin and guilt haunt you, try tears.

The Lamb of God
John 1:29

INTRODUCTION

Today, before we observe the Lord's Supper, let's consider the title *The Lamb of God*, the most striking in the Bible. John uses this to introduce the saving nature of the ministry of Christ.

John the Baptist was the last of the prophetic line. He didn't go to Jerusalem to preach; he made the town come out to hear him. His dress and diet were peculiar—he was clothed in camel's hair and ate locusts and wild honey. Using the banks of the Jordan for a platform, the gurgling stream behind him as a choir, and the open air spaces as an auditorium, he began to thunder, *"Repent, for the Kingdom of Heaven is at hand!"*

He became the Master of Ceremonies in this drama of redemption. He introduced Jesus to the crowd and to the world. They understood his language. The people had followed the custom of the slaying of a lamb and the High Priest going into the Holy of Holies to offer the blood of the lamb on the altar to atone or cover their sins.

Now John, seeing Jesus approaching, said, *"Look! Behold the Lamb of God who takes away the sin of the world!"* What John the Baptist said was "good news" because in this statement he revealed three new things concerning the saving ministry of the Lord Jesus Christ.

1. First, He was the Lamb of God. This was new. They had been offering their own lambs. Here was the appearance of God's Lamb.
2. Second, the Lamb took away sin. This was new. The lambs that they offered only covered sin. The Lamb of God, Jesus, did not just cover sin. He took it away.
3. Third, the Lamb of God took away the sin of the world. This was new. The Jewish lamb atoned only for the Hebrew nation. God's Lamb covered the world.

Now let's take notice of these three new things.

THE LAMB OF GOD

John announced, "Behold God's Lamb!" Revelation tells us that He is the Lamb who was slain before the foundation of the world.

1. We note from the Old Testament that an important day on the Jewish calendar was the Day of Atonement.
2. Year after year, when the Hebrew people killed the lamb, they were getting ready for the coming of Christ. They slew the lamb to cover their sins.
3. The lamb in the Old Testament had to have three qualifications:
   a. The lamb must be young.
   b. The lamb must be a male.
   c. The lamb must be perfect.

Now we see why Jesus, a male, died at thirty-three years and was sinless. However, let me remind you that the Lamb of God, Jesus, had to go to the cross in order to become our Savior. In the Hebrew home, the night of the Passover was never forgotten. On that day Moses told the people to slay a lamb and put the blood on the doorpost. Salvation came to the Hebrew home when the lamb was slain.

Paul said in Romans, *"Being justified freely by His blood, we have redemption."* The writer of Hebrews tells us, *"Without the shedding of blood there is no remission of sin."* 1 John 1:4 – *The blood of Christ cleanses us from all sin.*

SIN TAKEN AWAY

1. Here is the second new thing that John told us about God's Lamb. He takes away sin.
2. In the Old Testament the dead sacrifices did not take away sin; they just covered it.
3. This is the meaning of the Day of Atonement.
4. In Hebrew, it is *Yom Kippur*, meaning Day of Atonement.
5. The sins of the Old Testament saints were covered. When Adam sinned, it was covered. When Noah got drunk, his sin was covered. When Lot sinned, it was covered. All lies and dishonesty, all sins, were covered.
6. But when Jesus died, He did not cover our sins. He took them away.
7. The Bible tells us, *"As far as the east is from the west, so far has He removed our transgressions from us."*

8. There is a fountain filled with blood,
   Drawn from Immanuel's vein,
   And sinners plunged beneath that flood
   Lose all their guilty stain.

   What can wash away my sin?
   Nothing but the blood of Jesus.

   Yes, the good news is that He takes away our sin.

THE SIN OF THE WORLD

1. Notice in the Old Testament how the concept of sacrifice was expanded:
   a. In Abel's day, it was one lamb for **one man**.
   b. Later, on the night of the Passover, Moses instructed the family to put the blood on the doorpost, and the promise was, *"When I see the blood, I will pass over you."* Here is the sacrifice of one lamb for **one family**.
   c. Later, as God's people journeyed from Egypt to Canaan, they instituted a Day of Atonement. The High Priest gathered the entire nation together, went into the Holy of Holies, and made the sin sacrifice on the altar for the entire nation. This was one lamb for **one nation**.
   d. But now John the Baptist declares that the Lamb of God takes away the sin of **the entire world**. Salvation was available for

everyone. John 3:16 – *For God so loved Clarence Stewart* (one man), *for God so loved the world* (all men) *that He gave His only begotten Son that whosoever* (put your name in when we come to the word "whosoever") *believes in Him will not perish but have everlasting life.* Remember the hymn *He Included Me.* You are included by faith in Christ.

CLOSING

A man was once traveling through a midwestern town and came to a beautiful church with a steeple. On the steeple was a figure of a lamb. The passerby thought it strange, but upon inquiring from townsfolk he heard from them this story:

When the church was being built, a worker on the steeple fell from this high position. A man was passing below with a herd of sheep, and the falling worker landed on one of the lambs. The innocent animal broke the fall and saved the man. But the lamb died. The worker was so grateful that he climbed back up the steeple and placed there a figure of a lamb in memory of the lamb that saved him.

We have been saved by the Lamb of God, Jesus. Place Him in your heart now in memory of your salvation. He is God's Lamb. He takes away sin. He deals with the sin of the world, including you.

REMINISCING
Susan Wise

As I sat down to write my contribution to *The Devil's Toolbox*, I "reminisced" by looking at and reading through a booklet lovingly compiled by my sister, Karen, in 1998, on the occasion of our parents' 50th anniversary. It consisted of wedding day recollections from Mother and Daddy, wedding announcements from the newspaper, and individual messages to our parents from my brothers, sister and me with the following lead-in: "On the occasion of your 50th wedding anniversary, I'd like to tell you..."

After the tears stopped flowing, I came to the conclusion there was absolutely no way I could "reminisce" without the help of my siblings. After all, we were all in this *together*! So we are going to reminisce for you *together*, sharing the exact words we wrote for our parents back in 1998, in this order — Scott, Randy, Karen, Susan.

Mom and Dad,

You have been married for 50 years and there is so much I want to say. It will never fit into this small write-up, and I will probably never find the words to express how I feel about you both. Please accept this as a small token of my love for you, and know that this doesn't scratch the surface.

It would be obvious to say that I owe everything I am to you both, but sometimes the most simple things are the most meaningful to say. From my demeanor, to my sense of humor and my compassion, I can trace everything about myself to you.

Besides leading me down the road to Christianity and instilling a love for God and all He has done, one of the most important aspects of my life that you've given me is a place to call home. In Dad's line of work staying in one place for more than 20 years is hard to do. It is simply a credit to both of you that your stay in Pulaski was so long.

I would venture to say that you didn't know Pulaski existed as you vowed to love and hold one another as long as you both live. But somehow God led you to this small town that I call home. Once here, you chose to bring another life into the world.

I just want you to know that your decision to come to Pulaski was the best thing that ever happened to me. If nothing else, it gave me the opportunity to meet Sarah. However, where I live would have never been important without the guidance and love I received from you. I can't ever remember needing anything -- not food or clothing, and especially not love.

I remember Moma's calm demeanor and a creative streak a mile wide. You just didn't tell Mary Lou that you didn't have anything to do. She'd whip you up a project in a heartbeat.

Moma, you always gave me a sense of freedom and individuality without making me feel like I was on my own. You allowed me to venture out and were always there when I invariably fell on my face. It was never "I told you so," but "Why not try it this way?"

I always felt like such a big kid, when I would ride the bus and sometimes even walk from Pulaski Elementary to the high school. And later when I would walk from Bridgeforth to the bank, I just knew I was the most grown up kid in my class.

I know that my willingness to venture out without a fear of failure is due to you.

Daddy, I would find it hard to believe if somebody told me there was a more fun-loving father in the world. I fondly remember basketball games in the driveway, trips to the Southeastern Conference Basketball Tournament and Vanderbilt football games.

Even though I wasn't a morning person, I could count on you most mornings to come in and roust me up with a tune and smile. And as a sleepy little boy riding to school with you (as you read the newspaper) I could count on a barrage of philosophic questions like, "Do you walk to school or carry your lunch?" I still don't know the answer to that one.

I also remember being at the church with you and watching sometimes as you counseled with people in need. I may not have understood exactly what was going on, but I knew that people were seeking you out for help and it made me proud.

You both did much more than bring me into the world and give me a place to call home. You gave me the tools necessary to make the most of this life. Now, Sarah and I couldn't ask anything more from you. Your support and help with our house has been indispensable. We always look forward to your visits and only regret that we are not able to see you as often as we would like.

I feel very fortunate to have had both of you in my life for 32 years and look forward to the years to come. Thank you, Moma and Daddy, for everything. I only wish I could give you back a fraction of what you've given me.

Love,
Scott

Mom and Dad,

On the occasion of your 50th wedding anniversary, I would like to tell you...

...how proud I am of you;

...how thankful I am for you;

...that you have taught me many wonderful things, most of them learned just by watching the way you interact in your marriage;

...that the most important of these lessons has been the art of compassion for each other and your children;

...that other lessons I have observed (and tried to imitate) are persistence, tolerance, forgiveness, respect, reverence to God, living in the present, learning from the past, preparing for the future, teamwork, dignity, humility, and a healthy sense of humor;

...that I remember fondly, and will cherish forever, family events such as Rook games, sporting excursions, Wednesday night spaghetti dinners, Saturday morning pancakes, sing-alongs around the piano, and delightful Christmases;

...that nothing (not years or miles, sickness or death) will ever diminish my love for you and my appreciation of you;

...and that someday, in heaven if not on earth, you will realize fully how much good you have done and will be in perfect peace together as you rest in your accomplishments.

You gave me life; then you showed me how to live. No son could ask for anything more.

I love both of you,

Randy

Dearest Mom and Dad,

I thank you for loving me even though I've been a bit different (that's an understatement, I know), for carrying on in loving me when I made it quite hard to do, and for not shaking me loose when I had to sort myself out.

I do love you both dearly, and you have always been there for me. I find my mind wandering now into the rooms we lived in and touched as we flourished as kids -- the dust we caught on cotton cloths as we polished furniture and the smell of steam in the iron as I picked pillow cases out of the ironing basket (because they were easiest to iron) and pressed them to freshness while lost in the latest soap on TV.

Thank you for making me strong -- for churning out a resilient soul who meandered before she found herself. The poem that follows is just a little of what I know: I love you Mom and Dad. Happy Fiftieth Anniversary!

Love,

Karen

Promises Kept

You loved each other well.
Your youthful smiles in marriage
tell the story--the promise
to be a family and share with the world
four lively child souls
who carry your promise on.

You accomplished that in
many ways--touches of love--
promises so rich, I will never
forget how they were formed
first by your devotion for each other.

Life opened in a promise
of love to me 41 years ago.
You never deserted me,
turned your back on me,
stopped loving me.
You've never broken the promise.

And I remember ...
a little tweed dress coat
buttoned against my neck
and riding on a carousel
that was inside a store.
I liked to sit on the swan-shaped slick
seats or ride on ponies decorated in
enchanting paints.
The little man who pushed
the button to make the ride
propel itself round and round,
I remember him and Harvey's carousel rides.

I remember ...
opening a squatty refrigerator to a blast of
cold air and tucked inside was my Kool-Aid cup
verified with pink fingernail polish initials
stroked onto the bottom of clear plastic.
I remember Kool-Aid cups and the fun it
was to have them like I was part of
a Kool-Aid commercial.

I remember ...
visits to Kentucky,
rides into dizziness on Pappaw's green-speckled
swivel chair in his basement office.
"One for the money, two for the show,
three to get ready and four to go."
We would spin in delight.
I remember Pappaw's swivel chair.

I remember ...
the taste of cold turkey cooked in
Mammaw Lucy's huge roaster
then kept juicy in the fridge.
I'd sneak a piece as I headed to
the basement to ride the swivel chair.
I remember Mammaw Lucy's turkey.

I remember ...
the bottle of Absorbine Junior that
stayed in Lucy and Pappaw's medicine cabinet,
the squishy sponge top,
the green medicine inside the bottle,
and the "get better" smell.
I remember Absorbine Junior at
Lucy and Pappaw's.

I remember ...
The smell of apples as you crossed
the gate at Mammaw Pauline's house.
Her saying, "I'll get the divan out directly."
"Do you want something to eat?"
and the smell of Avon, the mix of
cardboard boxes and cosmetics.
Heating water in heavy pots for baths.
The cellar, Ghost in the Graveyard,
and Ice Cream and Lemonade
"Get to work and work all day."
I remember Mammaw Pauline's house.

I remember ...
Christmas at Mammaw Pauline's, too.
Her silver tree and icicles dangling.
Waking on Christmas morn to
a pink makeup kit that zipped and had
a picture of a little girl on front,
and two princess telephones for two
little girl princesses.
We hopped onto the soft mattress
where Mom and Dad slept--our gifts in tow.
I remember Christmas at Mammaw Pauline's.

I remember ...
Barrett's Creek.
A tiny church and scent of
polished wood. Hand-held fans with
the face of Jesus and the disciples
at The Lord's Supper.
Hymnals with weird shaped notes.
Blackberry pickin' at the
parsonage and the strangest
potty I've ever seen.
The pump and water with

the most distinct bouquet.
Revivals and trips to the
Dairy Cheer afterwards.
I remember Barrett's Creek.

I remember ...
Mr. Speck's garden and how
Dad owned part of it just by
throwing something into it.
Playing under the maple on
a quilt for hours.
I remember the shirt factory
whistle signaling the rhythm of
life within our days.
I remember rattails hanging
from the ceiling in our bedroom,
socials at Standing Stone Park
"When you come to the end of a lollipop,"
or "Tell me why the stars do shine."
I remember Beatles snowmen
and my own professional Barbie clothes designer,
tangerines and nuts in our Christmas stockings,
and finding a live tree each year.
I remember my childhood in Livingston.

I remember ...
Lincoln Street and Glendale Circle.
Bonfires and sleigh rides.
Pete the Skunk
Bootsie and R.B. Jr.
Andy and Fritz.
Jumping ocean waves with Dad while
on vacation as we made
a human chain across the ocean.
Davy Crockett pool trips and
corn dogs from the refreshment stand.

*Vacation Bible School Parades through town.
The Stewart Restaurant (leftovers night when
you got to pick what you wanted to eat from a menu).
Wednesday night prayer meetings and
finishing my homework in the church office.
I remember growing up at Lincoln and Glendale.*

*This is a sampler of memory,
of promises made and kept,
because two people loved each other
enough to bring four little lives
into a world, and loved enough
to always be there for them,
and for one another,
no matter what.*

*I remember ...
those two people.
I call them Mom and Dad.
I call myself lucky they are my parents.
Their vows of love whispered fifty years ago
will stay in the keeping room
of my heart forever
because I remember ...
promises kept.*

MOTHER AND DADDY,

ON THE OCCASION OF YOUR 50TH ANNIVERSARY, I WOULD LIKE TO TELL YOU:

>   WHAT YOU MEAN TO ME –
>   LIFE ITSELF (WITHOUT YOU I'M NON-EXISTENT)
>
>   WHAT YOU'VE TAUGHT ME –
>   LOVE (FOR GOD, OTHERS AND MYSELF)

> WHAT YOU'VE GIVEN ME –
> YOURSELF (AGAIN AND AGAIN AND AGAIN ....)
>
> WHAT I WILL PASS ON TO MY CHILDREN –
> LOVE OF HOME, FAMILY, CHURCH, MUSIC, ICE SKATING, FOOTBALL, BASEBALL, BASKETBALL, TRAVELING, KNOWLEDGE, FUN, FOOD AND FELLOWSHIP!

OBVIOUSLY, MY WORDS ARE INADEQUATE, BUT FORTUNATELY I CAN BORROW WORDS FROM SOMEONE WITH THE SAME PROBLEM --

> HOW CAN I SAY THANKS
> FOR THE THINGS YOU HAVE DONE FOR ME?
> THINGS SO UNDESERVED, YET YOU GIVE
> TO PROVE YOUR LOVE FOR ME.
> THE VOICES OF A MILLION ANGELS
> COULD NOT EXPRESS MY GRATITUDE --
> ALL THAT I AM AND EVER HOPE TO BE,
> I OWE IT ALL TO THEE.
> TO GOD BE THE GLORY, TO GOD BE THE GLORY!
> TO GOD BE THE GLORY FOR THE THINGS HE HAS DONE!

I CAN THINK OF NO GREATER TRIBUTE TO YOU THAN TO GIVE GOD THE GLORY FOR BRINGING YOU TOGETHER 50 YEARS AGO AND SEEING YOU THROUGH EACH DAY SINCE.

> I LOVE YOU AND THANK GOD FOR YOU!
>
> SUSAN

That last section sums it all up as far as I'm concerned. I can never thank my parents enough! I can never thank my God enough!

TO GOD BE THE GLORY FOR THE THINGS HE HAS DONE!

FOR FROM HIM AND THROUGH HIM AND TO HIM ARE ALL THINGS. TO HIM BE GLORY FOREVER! –Roman 11.38 NIV

Suffering

Fear Not! Don't Be Afraid
2 Timothy 1:7

INTRODUCTION

Sometime ago a Sunday School teacher asked her class members what they feared most. Their responses were revealing:

1) Not rearing my child correctly
2) Dying
3) Having cancer
4) Being attacked by dogs
5) Talking in front of others
6) Losing my family
7) Losing my job
8) Being unloved by God

I was in the barber's shop last week. Barbershops are like ladies' hair salons. You can find out about many things. In my shop they were fearful:

1) Fear of not having enough money to live
2) Fear of the direction America's going
3) Fear of the international scene
4) Fear of the future
5) Fear of robbers (a church had just been robbed)

How many of us could say "I have no fears" in a world that is trembling with apprehension and anxiety? How thankful we are that God in His wisdom helps us to deal with fear! From Genesis through Revelation there are ninety-nine times that it says, *"Fear not!"*

There are two kinds of fears that we face:

1) There is a wholesome, beneficial kind of

fear. We should be afraid to violate the laws of human nature and the laws of God and the laws of the state. This is a healthy type of fear.

2) The other fear is destructive. It does all kinds of evil things to the body and mind. How can we live in a world such as ours without harmful fear of any kind? The answer is found in the command: *"Fear not!"* Ecclesiastes 12:13 – *Fear God and keep His commandments.* This is redemptive fear. It liberates from unwholesome fear and replaces it with faith, peace, and assurance. The Psalmist exclaimed, *"I sought the Lord. He heard me and delivered me from all my fears"* (34:4). The fear of God is really not fear at all. I believe it is reverence, love, trust, and a deep desire to please. It brings us into God's inner presence, into His providence and protection, where we can say with confidence: *"I will fear no evil, for Thou art with me."* Such a relationship with God grows into *"perfect love that casts our all fear."*

There are definite ways whereby we can cooperate with God in removing every harmful fear from our hearts and mind.

WE CAN LIVE IN THE COMPANIONSHIP OF JESUS

We can practice His presence in our daily walk. In the consciousness of His presence all fear vanishes.

1) Jesus helps to conquer our fears.
2) Read John 6:16ff (Jesus walking on water).

3) I must confess that when I was a child I was afraid of the dark. It is nothing to be ashamed of. Even adults are afraid sometimes of water, spiders, and high places. We all are afraid sometime.

4) When Jesus walked on the water, His disciples heard Him say, *"It is I. Do not be afraid."*

5) The Bible tells us when they realized that it was Jesus they were willing to invite Him into the boat with them. They were fearful no longer.

6) When it comes to being fearful, we are all in the same boat. But when we invite Jesus into our boat, we have nothing to fear.

WE CAN GIVE ALL KNOWN FEARS OVER TO JESUS

1) We can confess our fears.

2) We can renounce them.

3) We can place them in Jesus' hands one by one.

4) We can ask Him to dispose of them, and He will.

5) Many fears can be overcome by courage and determination, but others may require a major operation of the Holy Spirit.

6) When we ask Him to remove them and we place ourselves completely in His hands, He will not fail.

7) All of us may be able to lose our great and persistent fears on our knees.

8) John Wesley was coming to America with a group of Moravians when a storm arose on the sea. Wesley was afraid. The Moravians prayed, sang hymns, and remained calm. Wesley learned that the Lord that we worship and serve can calm the waters. God can control the sea.

WE CAN APPLY THE WORD OF GOD TO EVERY FEAR THAT ARISES

There is a spiritual remedy for each fear. Find the passage that meets your need. Dwell on it! Store it in your mind! Repeat it often. Clasp it in your heart.

Faith can be substituted for fear, just like shifting gears in your cars. Simply by focusing your mind on the Word of God, the following verses will be helpful in combating some of the most common fears:

1) INSECURITY: Philippians 4:19 – *My God shall supply all your needs.*

2) DANGER: Psalm 91:11 – *He will give His angels orders concerning you to protect you in all your ways.*

3) FAILURE: Isaiah 41:13 – *I, the Lord your God, will help you.*

4) TROUBLE: Psalm 46:1 – *God is our refuge and strength.*

5) IN TIME OF WAR: Psalm 27:1-3 – *The Lord is my light and my salvation; whom shall I fear? The Lord is the strength of my life; whom shall I dread? When evildoers came upon me to devour my flesh, my adversaries and my enemies, they stumbled and fell. Though a*

host encamps against me, in spite of this I shall be confident.

6) THE FUTURE: Psalm 23:6 – *Surely goodness and mercy will follow me all the days of my life.*

7) DEATH: Psalm 23:4 – *Though I walk through the valley of the shadow of death, I will fear no evil, for Thou art with me.*

The Word of God covers every need in the happenings of life. To search these verses out, to claim them as your own, and to cherish them in your minds and hearts is to possess the marvelous resources of Heaven here on earth and to live above the reach of fear.

CLOSING

A girl was afraid of riding through tunnels. She overcame the fear by herself. "How?" her mother asked. "Because I realized there was light at both ends."

The Light is the Lord. Don't be afraid!

How to Rejoice
Philippians 4:4

INTRODUCTION

Thomas Watson said, "There are two things that I have always looked upon as difficult: (1) to make the wicked sad; (2) to make the godly joyful."

Most Christians would agree with the first but find it difficult to accept the second. Yet surely the radiance of happiness and overflowing joy is missing in many Christians. It is true that the gospel centers in a cross and the New Testament was soaked in martyr's blood, yet we only need to read the New Testament and early church records to see:

1. Christians triumphed in persecution, and their theme was irrepressible joy.
2. The first Christians ate their food *"with gladness and singleness of heart."*
3. Paul, from prison to prison, had an attitude of rejoicing.
4. Simon Peter implored a church that faced fiery trials to *"rejoice with joy unspeakable and full of glory."*

The emotion of joy was not outlawed among the saints in those days. Truly, those early Christians did not endure their Christianity; they enjoyed it.

But what about us? The first Christians had problems. Today, we have problems. Do we have holy joy? Today, the average Christian is more circumstance-centered than Christ-centered and feels that if all personal problems could be removed, he or she would be happy forever. And yet we know that real joy and peace is much deeper.

I remind you that the book of Philippians is the "joy book" of the Bible, written by a man under pressure and opposition because of his faith and devotion to his Lord. Logic says that such a man should complain, but this man, because of his faith, had a spirit of gratitude, joy, peace, praise, and spiritual anticipation. Paul is writing to the Christians at Philippi and to us to explain how we might experience real joy. In today's Scripture verse, he gives the Philippians three words of admonition:

1. Notice the **stress on rejoicing**: *again and again.* He recognized the importance of continual gratitude, praise, and joy.
2. Notice the **source of rejoicing**: *in the Lord.* We do not rejoice in circumstances, feelings, the weather, or the attitudes of others toward us, but in the Lord.
3. Notice the **season of rejoicing**: *always.* Are we to rejoice only when good things are happening, or should this be a constant attitude? Paul says *always.*

This verse is as much a commandment of the Lord as the Ten Commandments in the Old Testament, and yet many Christians are daily disobeying it.

OBSTACLES TO REJOICING

1. **Secret sin.** If you are harboring sins in your life that no one knows about but you and God, you are still guilty, and these sins keep you out of fellowship with the Lord. When David sinned, he said, *"Restore to me the joy of my salvation."* Unconfessed sin keeps us from having joy.
2. **Doubting God.** Our Heavenly Father would never cause us as His children to doubt, and

if we are experiencing this, it is because of Satan's work on our lives. God grieves when He sees a lack of faith in our lives. The Bible says, *"Without faith it is impossible to please God."* Doubting produces no joy.
3. **Lack of gratitude.** Daily blessings hinder our ability to experience spiritual joy. Young people fail to appreciate their parents. Husbands fail to appreciate their wives. Wives fail to appreciate their husbands. Employers fail to appreciate their employees. Little children, when they pray, usually thank God for everything. There is something beautiful and special about a little child's spirit of gratitude toward God.
4. **Neglecting spiritual disciplines.** Daily Bible reading, prayer, worship, and witnessing are vital if we are to be obedient. If we fail in these areas, it is impossible for us to experience God's best in our lives.
5. **Unresolved broken relationships.** Perhaps you had an argument with a member of your family or with someone at work, in your neighborhood, or at church. You said things you regret, and now the mere mention of that person's name creates a spirit of resentment.

OPPORTUNITIES FOR REJOICING

1. **Rejoice in the problems of life.** James 1:2 says, *"Consider it all joy, my brethren, when you experience various trials."* The writer is actually encouraging us to rejoice when problems come our way, just as the early Christians did. Anyone can be excited when something good happens, but the test of spiritual maturity is our ability to praise God

in the midst of a problem.
2. **Rejoice in the prosperity of other Christians.** Romans 12:15 says, *"Rejoice with them that rejoice and weep with them that weep."* It's easy for us to weep with those who have sorrow, but the Christian often finds it hard to rejoice with those who have prosperity. A neighbor gets a new car. Someone gets a job you wanted. A relative moves into a new home. A young person excels in music or sports. A girl is crowned for her beauty and charm. Does this make you happy, and are you able to rejoice with them? Learn to be glad when something good happens to someone else and not be envious.
3. **Rejoice in the preaching of the gospel.** Philippians 1:18 says, *"What then, only that in every way, whether in pretense or in truth, Christ is proclaimed. And in this I rejoice; yes, and I will rejoice."* Whenever Christ is preached, we must rejoice in it.

OUTCOME OF REJOICING

1. **Our physical health will be improved.** Doctors have stated that much of the illness of people today is caused by psychosomatic problems that stem from a bad attitude toward God, self, or others. In contrast, when we learn the principle of rejoicing, it affects our health in a positive way. Notice the people who always seem to feel bad physically. They often have an attitude problem. They complain, gripe, and always have something negative to say about any situation. It makes good sense for every Christian to praise God daily.

2. **Others will be blessed.** Psalm 40:3 states, *"And He hath put a new song in my mouth, even praise unto God. Many shall see and fear and shall trust in the Lord."* Everyone enjoys being around people who have a bright, joyful attitude toward life.
3. **Your life and outlook will change.** You will have abounding optimism.

The Ministry of Encouragement
1 Thessalonians 5:11

[11]*Therefore encourage one another and build up one another, just as you also are doing.*

INTRODUCTION

Dr. Thomas Harris, in his book *I'm OK, You're OK*, says that 96% of the population does not have "OK" feelings about themselves. According to Harris, most people struggle with feelings of inferiority. Most are easily discouraged, and this discouragement is reflected in the lives of people in the Church. Family situations, strained relationships, wrong lifestyles, failures, disappointments, and hurts produce discouragement, and faith wavers.

Today's message centers on ways we can strengthen people in their faith by encouraging them. In Acts 4:36 there was a man by the name of Barnabas, which means *Son of Encouragement.* He was an encourager. In three passages in the book of Acts we note his spirit:

1) In Acts 4:33-37 he helped and encouraged others by selling his own property and giving to the needy. He lifted the spirits of those in need.

2) After Paul was saved on the Damascus Road (Acts 9:26-27), he was not received well. Barnabas stood up for him, encouraging those who heard him to listen and standing with him as he proclaimed truth.

3) In Acts 15:36 Barnabas encouraged John Mark, his nephew, by standing with him when Paul did not want Mark to be on the

team because he had left the group on the first missionary journey. Barnabas stood with him and inspired Mark with his courage. He took him with him on his journey to Cyprus. Indeed, he was an encourager.

Now let me share with you from God's Word two areas or ways we can strengthen others in the faith. But remember: just being in Christ is a source of encouragement.

DISCIPLE BELIEVERS (Acts 11:19-26)

1) This passage flashes back to the persecution initiated by Saul after Stephen's death.

2) This persecution scattered the believers after Stephen's death.

3) Believers spread to Phoenicia, Cyprus, and still others to Antioch.

    a. They preached the Word to the Jews.

    b. Believing Jews then spoke to the Greeks.

    c. The believers who preached at Antioch were Greek-speaking Jews, including Barnabas.

4) As they preached, the hand of the Lord came upon them, and many believed.

5) The church in Jerusalem got reports about what was happening.

6) Barnabas was sent by the Jerusalem church to investigate. He is described as a good man, full of God's Spirit and of faith.

7) Barnabas encouraged the Antioch believers (verse 23):

a. He saw the grace of God in them.
   b. He was glad for them.
   c. He encouraged them to cleave to the Lord.

8) Barnabas left to go to Tarsus to find Paul. He brought Paul to Antioch, and they preached and taught for one year.

9) The disciples were first called *Christians* at Antioch.

HELP PEOPLE TO LEARN ABOUT CHRIST
(Acts 13:14-15; 42-43)

1) Acts 13:1-3 tells how the Lord called two key leaders of the Church: Barnabas and Saul.

2) These two men were sent to Asia Minor to preach the gospel. They went into the synagogues of the cities on the Sabbath.

3) Men, if you have a word of encouragement or exhortation, share it!

4) They preached to the Jews (verses 16-41). This is the longest sermon recorded in Acts.

5) In the sermon, Paul reviewed the history under David's reign. Then he explained that through David's descendants God brought the Savior to Israel. He explained how this fulfilled the Scriptures, and he ended with a warning not to reject God's clear revelation.

6) After the meeting, people begged Paul and Barnabas to tell more truth, persuading them to continue to share the message of God's grace in their city.

7) We too can reach out to unbelievers to help them to learn about Christ.

Comfort One Another
1 Thessalonians 4:18

[18] *Therefore comfort one another with these words.*

- Bear one another's burdens
- Prefer one another
- Forgive one another
- Love one another
- Receive one another
- Edify one another

INTRODUCTION

In the movies we are often moved with compassion or anger. But sometimes in life we are not moved by what is going on with those around us. Yet we are commanded to "comfort one another."

THE SOURCE OF THE COMFORT
(2 Corinthians 1:3)

1. God is the source – No one can comfort like God. The people of the world may try to comfort, but what the world has to offer simply doesn't hold up.

2. Jesus is the messenger – Jesus said, *"I will not leave you comfortless"* (John 14:18). The world says, "Everything will be alright. Just give it time." Jesus says, *"Cheer up! I have overcome the world."*

3. The Holy Spirit is the Comforter.
4. God uses us as Christians to represent Him in the comfort of others. He uses us to comfort.

THE SCOPE OF COMFORT

1. Foundational to God's comfort is His commitment to provide. *"The Lord is my Shepherd,"* David said, *"I shall not want."* Our needs are going to be met because Jesus is the Shepherd of our lives.
2. David said, *"Thy rod and Thy staff they comfort me."*
    A. The rod was used by shepherds to defend their sheep against an outside attack. The rod represents God's capacity to protect.
    B. The staff is a thin pole with a crook on the end of it. The staff was used by the shepherd to hook the leg of a straying sheep and put it back on the right course. Therefore the staff represents God's capacity to direct. God comforts us as He protects and directs. Paul's experience illustrates this in 2 Corinthians 7:5-6. It's not an easy path.
    C. God's comfort does not fade.
       (2 Thessalonians 2:16)
    D. God's comfort lasts.
       (Revelation 21:4, Isaiah 66:13)

THE PURPOSE OF OUR COMFORT

Blessed are they who mourn, for they shall be comforted." – Matthew. 5:4

The real purpose of comfort is to reveal who God is and who we can become. When God says, "I will comfort," He does so through...

1. **Salvation** – He takes away guilt and helps us to like ourselves again (Isaiah. 1:18).
2. **Rescue from temptation** – He catches us when we stumble and puts us back on the right track.
3. **Sanctification** – Through us, the world can see the difference God can make. He conforms us to His image (John16:8-11).

THE MEANS OF COMFORT

Job 16 – Job called his three friends *miserable comforters*.

1. How not to give comfort

    A. **Don't assume.** – Eliphaz, Bildad and Zophar assumed the reason for Job's suffering was sin (Job 4:7) and tried to get Job to acknowledge it.

    B. **Don't just listen to words.** – Be alert to feelings (Job 7:11). His friends examined everything he said but had missed his hurt and his feelings.

    C. **Don't say what you don't know.** – Job's friends waxed eloquent in their counsel. What they said was good. Their mistake was attempting to show another person how he made his mistake without first establishing if, in fact, he had made one.

    D. **Don't underestimate the human heart.** Some comfort is superficial when the problem is not.

2. How we should give comfort

   A. **We must receive God's comfort before we can give it** (2 Corinthians 1:3-4).

   B. **The ministry of Christian comfort must be reciprocal** (Romans 1:12). Everybody is to both give and receive comfort. Comfort one another. Open up and share.

   C. **The one who comforts must identify with the hurt.** Paul said (Romans 12:15): *"Rejoice with them that do rejoice and weep with them that weep."* Christian comfort is best received from a person who knows what hurt is. Illustration: Jesus was *a man of sorrows.* Jesus hurt. Paul knew *"how to be abased."* He knew what it was to hurt. Put yourself in the person's shoes.

   D. **Comfort must be given from the Word.** Romans 15:4 talks about the comfort of the Scripture.

   E. **We need not only the Word but also the Spirit.** Under the power of the Spirit the Word was written. And it's only under the power of the Spirit that the Word is acted upon. Counseling is not giving a word back like a parakeet but giving guidance by the Paraclete (*Paraclete = Spirit* in the Greek). Don't exclude the Spirit. No question about it – life isn't easy. Many people are hurting. I pray that you will be one who comforts and consoles through the Bible in the power of the Spirit.

Loving Promises for Lonely People
John 15:15, 16:7

INTRODUCTION

It was near the end of Jesus' earthly ministry. Very soon the disciples would be left to face a hostile world alone. At times they would be discouraged. At times they would be lonely. Anticipating these days, Jesus speaks to them wonderful words of comfort and assurance. *"Henceforth,"* He says, *I have called you friends"* (John 15:15).

Loneliness can be a desperate experience. Years ago Admiral Richard E. Byrd went to Little America to make scientific observations of the polar region. For six months he lived absolutely alone in a station that had been built for that purpose. During that time he saw no other face; he heard no other voice except by short wave radio. Upon returning home, he wrote a vivid account of his isolation at the South Pole under the simple title *Alone*.

Not many people experience such a prolonged period of solitude. Millions, however, (and at times all of us) experience some degree of loneliness.

    A. There is the loneliness of those who, deprived of family life, live by themselves.

    B. There is the loneliness of missionaries far from loved ones.

    C. There is the loneliness of young people away from home.

        a. Some in military service
        b. Some in college
        c. Some starting out on their own

- D. There is the loneliness of wife and children separated from husband and father, the loneliness of parents as sons and daughters get married and leave home.
- E. There is the loneliness of the sick room.
- F. There is the loneliness of the bereaved, separated from a loved one whose companionship has meant everything across the years.
- G. There is the loneliness of the aged, feeling unwanted and in the way.
- H. There is the loneliness of our youth going off to college.

Yes, loneliness is one of the real problems in life for many, many people.

JESUS EXPERIENCED THIS PROBLEM OF LONELINESS

- A. He knew about it right in His own home. One of the tragedies of His earthly life was that His own brothers and at times even His own mother did not understand Him. John said, *"He came unto His own, and His own received Him not."*
- B. Jesus knew the loneliness of the wilderness when He was tempted forty days by the devil.
- C. He knew loneliness of being deserted. (He stood for principles.)
- D. There was the deep loneliness of Gethsemane. If ever He wanted someone to stand by Him, He wanted it then. He

took with Him three men on whom He thought He could most depend. Yet they slept while He was having His agonizing experience.

E. And there was the awful loneliness of the cross, when for a moment it seemed as if God Himself had deserted Him. All the agony of all the lonely hearts in the world was caught up in that cry, *"My God, My God, why hast Thou forsaken Me?"* Sometimes we, too, know the loneliness and agony of saying, "My God, why?"

LONELINESS IS AN OLD PROBLEM

A. There are times when we need to be alone.
   a. To think
   b. To pray
   c. To be with Jesus

B. Each of us should be the kind of person who is appropriate when he is alone. Edgar Guest, in his poem *Myself*, said, "I have to live with myself, and so I want to be fit for myself." A little girl was asked why she was talking to herself. She answered, "Because I'm nice to talk to." Are you nice to talk to when you are alone?

C. We are so made that we do need human friendship and are desperately unhappy without it.

   1. Luke gives us an unusual picture of Paul in Acts 28:15. When believers visited Paul during his imprisonment, *"he thanked God*

and took courage."

2. Happy is the person who has loved ones and friends to give love and encouragement.

3. Yet many do not have friends.

4. One part of the mission of the Church is to show friendship to the lonely, to throw Her arms around the unloved and the unwanted until they feel welcome in the sight of God and within the Christian fellowship. Everybody is somebody.

YET THE BIBLE GOES DEEPER THAN MERE HUMAN FRIENDSHIP

1. The Old Testament says in Proverbs 18:24, *"There is a friend who sticks closer than a brother."*

2. The New Testament capitalizes the word *"Friend"* and presents Jesus as the perfect Friend.

3. Remember, Jesus said, *"Henceforth I no longer call you servants, but I have called you friends."*

4. No wonder we sing "Jesus, What a Friend of Sinners" and "What a Friend We Have in Jesus"! When God walked the earth in the person of Jesus, He came not as a foe but as a friend. And life, with its human friendships, is never fully satisfied until contact is made with this *"Friend who stays closer than a brother."*

It is all important to know Him, for there are

times when all of us must walk alone. We all must experience loneliness. Sometimes we must go down into some valley of decision where not even a wife or husband can go with us all the way. We must make decisions alone. Sometimes we must go through the valley of suffering and pain alone. And one day we will go on the loneliest journey of all, through the valley of the shadow of death.

When we go into the valley of decision, we do not go alone. One is there to guide us. When we walk into the valley of pain, we do not go alone. One who knows all about suffering is there to sustain us. When we walk into the valley of the shadow of death, we need not go alone. One who knows the way has promised to be with us—One who does not call us servants but friends—the greatest Friend: **Jesus Christ.**

Rejoice in the Trials of Our Faith
James 1:2

²*Consider it all joy, my friends, when you encounter various trials.*

I will share a personal word today. Anyone can be excited when something good happens. But a test of spiritual maturity is our ability to praise God in the midst of a problem.

In early December of 1985, I was elected to serve as Partnership Mission Consultant of the Tennessee Baptist Convention. The last Sunday in December I resigned my church, effective the last Sunday of January.

The next day after I had submitted my resignation, I had surgery for a throat problem. I did not get the report from my surgery until New Year's Day. Randy, my son, who was in his medical residency in Birmingham, called me.

"Dad," he said, "I got your surgery report. There is bad news and good news. The bad news is that you have a malignancy of the throat. The good news is that the problem can be arrested through radiation treatment. Dad, the God you have been preaching about for years is able to provide healing."

Needless to say, I was hurt and crushed by this news. But I was helped by his words of encouragement. I could not sleep that night. My wife and I talked into the early hours of the morning.

I began my radiation therapy January 12, 1986. My final sermon at my church was the last

Sunday of January. The therapy affected my voice and speaking. After thirty-one treatments, I was unable to preach again until April 20, 1986. It was in a revival meeting in Siluria, Alabama. My first evangelistic visit in the revival effort was with a man who had lung cancer. I could identify with him. We had a similar problem. What a thrill for me to lead him to a personal commitment to Christ! What a joy came to his heart that day! Rejoice? Yes, I did.

My first trip to Venezuela in the partnership was in July, 1986. It was a thrill to preach Christ and see the people respond to His invitation. At the victory service following the crusade in Caracas, I told the congregation that in the midst of a health problem God had permitted me to proclaim His saving message.

We have trials in our spiritual journeys. These problems are difficult and hurtful to us. Yet, as the Scripture admonishes, we must learn to rejoice even in these situations, knowing that God's goodness and grace will be manifested.

So today – *Rejoice in the Lord; and again I say, "Rejoice!"*

Never Lose Heart
2 Corinthians 4:8-18

INTRODUCTION

     I received a letter from a man named J.D. I also received a call from a friend in another city. I have talked with other friends as well who have shared the same message: "I am about ready to give up." We all know what it is to lose heart—from others' experience and from our own experience.

     Paul had reason to lose heart:

Five times I received from the Jews forty lashes minus one. Three times I was beaten with rods. Once I was stoned. Three times I was shipwrecked. I have spent a night and a day in the depths of the sea.
     – 2 Corinthians 11:24-25

Therefore, so that I would not exalt myself, a thorn in the flesh was given to me, a messenger of Satan to torment me so that I would not exalt myself. Concerning this, I pleaded with the Lord three times to take it away from me. – 2 Corinthians 12:7-8

     Now compare the above with this verse:

How will the ministry of the Spirit not be more glorious? For if the ministry of condemnation be glory, much more does the ministry of righteousness exceed in glory.
     – 2 Corinthians 3:8-9

WHY DOES THIS BOAST OF PAUL AMAZE US?

It amazes us because losing heart is so nearly universal. All sorts of people lose heart:
- the dull and stupid
- the wise and understanding
- the strong and the weak
- young and old
- the depressed and the suicidal

We lose heart over all sorts of things:
- the world scene
- the degeneration of morals in society
- the breakdown of the home
- physical problems
- disappointments with self and others
- tragedy and sorrow

Losing heart...
- slows us down
- kills the joy in our lives
- changes us from an asset to a liability for the cause of Christ

But Paul said, "I am knocked down but never knocked out."

PAUL KEPT A STOUT HEART. HOW DID HE DO IT?

Remember the foes he faced, and note the foes you face.
- Paul refused to lose heart in spite of **opposition**.
- Paul refused to lose heart in spite of **physical handicaps**.
- Paul refused to lose heart in spite of **failure**.

PAUL DID NOT GIVE UP

He kept heart because he had a genuine and growing experience with God:

All this is for your sakes...that the abundant grace of God may bring glory to God (verse 15).

Paul kept heart because he was constantly renewed and reinforced. God's grace was sufficient, giving him spiritual strength.

Paul refused to lose heart because he was sure of the victory. To Timothy, he wrote: *I have fought a good fight... I have kept the faith.* He knew that *"all things work together for good"* (Romans 8:28).

When you walk through the storm,
hold your head up high
And don't be afraid of the dark...
Walk on, walk on with hope in your heart,
And you'll never walk alone!
You'll never walk alone!

Remembering Loved Ones

INTRODUCTION

We are here this afternoon, as the living, to remember loved ones who have died in 2001. The staff of Cole and Garrett Funeral Home and I want you to know that our heartfelt sympathy and prayers continue for you in adjustment to your loss.

In the book of Psalms (chapter 30), David—the sweet singer of Israel, the man after God's own heart—had gone through the death of a son. He was facing a difficult, distressful time. David told how God had heard his prayer and brought comfort to him. Then David gives a promise: *"Weeping may endure for a night, but joy cometh in the morning."*

Indeed, when we lose a loved one in death, weeping will come. The loss of a family member is like a wound; the deeper the cut, the longer it takes to heal. Just so, the deeper the love, the deeper the grief and the longer the healing process.

There is a sense in which we never get over the loss of a loved one. However, in time we will heal. What can hasten and help the healing? What can bring joy in the morning?

I have four suggestions.

GOOD MEMORIES WILL BRING JOY IN THE MORNING

These memories focus on what you had more than what you lost. Remember the good times, the happy times. Remember the wonderful years together.

The old Stamps-Baxter hymn, *Precious Memories*, expresses it best:

> Precious memories, unseen angels,
>   sent from somewhere to my soul.
> How they linger, ever near me,
>   and the sacred past unfold!
> Precious memories, how they linger,
>   how they ever flood my soul!
> In the stillness of the midnight,
>   precious sacred scenes unfold.

Good memories will bring joy in the morning.

KEEPING BUSY WILL BRING JOY IN THE MORNING

When sorrow comes, it is so easy to sit down in despair and despondence. We should not do it. We should not linger in grief. We should get on with living. We should keep busy. We need to reach out to others who need help. Work can heal a lot of hurts and bring joy in the morning.

THE BIBLE'S PROMISE OF HEAVEN AND REUNION SHOULD BRING JOY IN THE MORNING

Peter Marshall's last words to his wife were, "See you, darling. See you in the morning."

THE GRACE OF GOD WILL HELP BRING JOY IN THE MORNING

In God's Word, God has promised grace sufficient. God comes to us in our deepest sorrow and provides grace that brings comfort and strength to our hearts. His grace can help us in times of weeping and bring hope, help, and joy in the morning.

CLOSING

Jesus had a lot to say about light. In John 8:12, he said, *"I am the Light of the world. He that follows Me shall not walk in darkness but shall have the light of life."*

Jesus reminds us that there is life and light in His Resurrection. Paul also reminds us (1 Corinthians 15:51-58) that the light shines even now because of the Resurrection.

The candles today are lit in remembrance of your family member, your loved one. Each represents that light of life. Now let us remember each one as I call the names.

Faithful and Flourishing
Psalm 92:12-15

12 *The righteous shall flourish like a palm tree;*
He shall grow like a cedar in Lebanon.
13 *Those who are planted in the house of the Lord*
Shall flourish in the courts of our God.
14 *They shall bear fruit in old age;*
They shall be fresh and flourishing,
15 *To declare that the Lord is upright;*
He is my rock, and there is no unrighteousness in Him.

INTRODUCTION

Note what the Psalmist said in verse 14.

There is one way to avoid old age – die young! It is perfectly normal to get older, but we treat it as a disease.

Today many people try to fight old age; they also camouflage it or deny it. Certainly, the later years of life do have some minuses.

A preacher in South Carolina made the statement that life after fifty is characterized by four B's: bulges, bifocals, baldness, and bridges. An older woman in the congregation said, "Preacher, don't forget my bunions!"

A woman said recently, "I have been completely happy since I stopped trying to look and act twenty years younger and began acting my age."

B.M. Kirkland said once, "Wrinkles are only the bypaths of many smiles and some tears; gray hair is the silver dust of the stars; and growing gracefully slower of step is only walking nearer and closer to God."

The senior years may not be as glamorous as the years before, yet the later years in life can be fun, interesting, and fruitful in many ways.

The advances of science have lengthened our lives. In 1950 the life expectancy for a woman had risen to 72 and for a man 67. Now there are about seventeen million people in the U.S. over 65. It is estimated that there will be more than twenty million in 1975.

Has science done us a favor in lengthening our life expectancy? Not necessarily, unless we learn to fill these added days with beauty, trust, usefulness, and love.

All too common today is the mistaken notion that to provide older folk with social security, a place to live, and plenty to eat is enough. But some of the loneliest people are those who draw the limit in social security, have a place to live and plenty to eat, and do a lot of traveling.

Senior citizens want more than just comfort and security. They want to be loved, needed, and useful. Life finds fulfillment when one has discovered a philosophy to live by and something to live for.

Throughout history, some people have found the secret:

- Moses enlisted for his job at 80.
- Caleb, at 80, wanted to fight for his inheritance in the Promised Land.
- John Wesley, at 71, traveled 4,500 miles a year by horseback helping people.
- Michelangelo was at his best at 70.
- Louis Pasteur's best achievements came after he was 60.

Someone has estimated that 64% of the world's greatest achievements have been made by people past sixty, 23% by people between seventy and eighty, and only 13% by people under forty.

Life ought to end flourishing and fruitful and not frustrated. I think we all would like to be like Paul. He came to the end of the way and said:

For I am already being poured like a drink offering, and the time for my departure is at hand. I have fought the good fight, I have finished the race, I have kept the faith. Now there is in store for me the crown of righteousness which the Lord, the righteous Judge, will award to me on that day – and not only to me, but also to all who have longed for His appearing.
2 Timothy 4:6-8.

Life makes demands on us, and as long as we meet them we never grow old. <u>We get old when we stop growing.</u>

This morning let me suggest to senior adults the secret of mastery of the later years of life.

NEVER STOP LEARNING

John Locke said, "It is a duty we owe to God to have our minds constantly open to receive and entertain new truth when we meet it."

Our bodies sag because our minds are already sagging. An elderly lady said recently, "There are three things I can't remember. I can't remember names; I can't remember faces; and I can't remember the third thing I can't remember."

John Wesley continued his studies in old age. Mary Lou, my wife, started taking piano lessons at 63.

It is a fallacy that a person cannot learn in later years. We take it for granted that memory fails us and we can't do anything about it. Ask questions. Be inquisitive. Never stop learning.

Jesus kept *"increasing in wisdom, stature, and in favor with God and man."* So should you.

KEEP UP WITH THE TIMES

How we hate change, especially as we get older! Senior adults have a favorite pastime: "I remember when..." Memories are wonderful, but they are merely the frosting on the cake and not the cake. I remind you that no one wants a steady diet of "I remember when..."

Changes are all about us. Changes make new development possible.

I heard about a salesman who approached a

farmer about buying a tractor. The farmer said, "For forty years I have been studying the tastes, the likes, and the dislikes of the mule, and I am not going to give up all that knowledge for any newfangled tractor."

Life is boring unless we keep up with the times. I don't mean that we should adopt every fad. We should know what is happening in the world. We should have opinions and make informed decisions. We should learn from the Boomers and the Busters.

KEEP BUSY

- Don't overwork, but keep busy at something you like to do—creative things, worthwhile contributions.

- When retirement comes, don't quit. The reason many people die after retirement is that they don't have anything useful to do to occupy their time.

- I question whether compulsory retirement at 65, regardless or health or ability, is right. If your company makes you retire at 65, be getting ready to go into something else.

- Continue to be involved in church; continue to care; continue to be leaders. Be good leaders.

- Every person can find things to do. It is important that we develop interests that will sustain us when retirement comes.

- My mother, who died at 87, sold Avon products until she was 85.
- Share your faith.

BELIEVE IN YOURSELF

It's fatal at any age to say, "I am not worth anything to anybody—God or man." <u>You are somebody. You are important.</u> Life has a worthwhile goal for each of us. We are made in God's image, and He needs us as long as we live. We may get restless because we cannot do some things we used to do. Remember this verse: Mark 9:23 – *All things are possible to him who believes.*

LIVE OUTSIDE YOURSELF

The tendency in later years is to get selfish and be concerned with only what concerns us. How desperately friends are needed in the senior years!

Charles Lamb complained that all his friends, his schoolmates, and his companions were gone. Samuel Johnson reminded him and us that "a person must keep his friendships in repair!"

To have friends, we must be friendly and be interested in other people and what interests them. Someone has said, "A person all wrapped up in himself makes a mighty small package."

Cultivate people. Live outside yourself.

Get along with others. Be cheerful. Don't be ornery, grumpy, or disagreeable.

Visit friends. Call people. Encourage young people. Witness. Do all you can do for your church.

LIVE CLOSE TO GOD

We need God all the time. But this is especially true in the final years of life. The person with a firm faith in God faces the senior adult years eagerly and without fear. How important it is to give ourselves to God early in life so that our companionship with God deepens as years go by!

Consider the story of two blind men. One, who was not a Christian, said, "I have no inner resource." To the other, going blind was not a curse. He said, "I am not afraid. I have a strong faith and some inner resources."

Build up inner resources. Have a growing trust in God. Zechariah 14:7 – *At evening time it shall be light.*

A noted Bible scholar, Dr. Walter Bowie, got a letter from a little boy who concluded the letter by saying, "Doctor, I hope you live all your life." That's it!

A great Japanese Christian prayed, "Lord, though my muscles stiffen, though my skin wrinkles, though my hair turns gray, may I never find myself yawning at life."

We must not run from life. We must live life with faith and trust in God.

SUMMARY

The secret of the mastery of the later years of one's life:

Never stop learning.

Keep up with the times.

Keep busy.

Believe in yourself.

Live outside yourself.

Live close to God.

God and the Church

The Old-Time Religion
Acts 8:5-8

INTRODUCTION

I received my call to the ministry in 1949. After my college and seminary training and two seminary pastorates, I became a fulltime pastor at First Baptist Church of Livingston, Tennessee. This was in 1957. Sometime afterward I became aware of the fast decline of what many have called the old-time religion. In my lifetime I have been aware of a new theology, a new morality, and even what some have called a new-time religion.

My pastor in childhood was a faithful preacher of the old-time way. I remember the two country churches I pastored in seminary days – hot summers with no air conditioning but only fans from the funeral homes; no meal inside a fellowship hall but rather dinner on the grounds; tables laden with delicious foods and flies kept away by the ladies of the church. I remember the revival meetings in July and August. The presence of the Lord was real and vital in the one to two weeks of preaching. There was enthusiastic singing of the great hymns of the church and hellfire and damnation preaching by the evangelists. The people were called back to God, sinners repented and got saved, and church members came to the altar confessing their sins.

Entire communities were turned on to Jesus. Christians went out from the revival to live and act differently. They reconciled one to another. If they had fallen out with their neighbor, they made things right. They made restitution if they had mistreated or taken advantage of others. The old-time religion found expression in the daily lives of the people. There was generosity, love, and kindness in the community. If a man broke his back or had other physical problems, they didn't put him on welfare. The community came together to cut his hay, plow his corn, feed his hogs, even taking the family to the market. They would say, "Don't worry. We will take care of you because we are your brothers in Christ."

However, in my lifetime I have seen these days pass. There has been a falling away from the old-time way. Today we have a new sophistication, a new morality, a new way of doing things. We come to worship on Sunday, and many go out and do as they please, living it up during the week. Some of the changes I have seen are:

1. different interpretations of the Bible
2. contemporary music
3. fewer and fewer revival meetings
4. liberals and other non-believers getting in the way of Jesus
5. humanism (man trying to save man) being advocated
6. large numbers becoming members of our churches yet fewer and fewer taking leadership roles and giving tithes and offerings to support the church
7. a lack of missionary vision in many congregations

On and on I could go, and you could add to the list. Let me state emphatically that I identify with the old-time religion, as many of you do. I feel there are some values we have lost through the years that we ought to reclaim.

Now let's turn to the text in Acts 8. A study in the book of Acts shows many aspects of the old-time religion. Philip went down to Samaria and preached Jesus Christ (vs. 4). They were in one accord (vs. 5). Miracles were wrought (vs. 6). There was great joy (vs. 8). Many were saved and baptized (vs. 12). Believers received the Holy Spirit (vs. 17). The old-time religion of Philip, Paul, and many preachers of the Church over the years is the message I proclaim today.

IT WAS A RELIGION OF THE **BIBLE**.

The old-time preacher never doubted the Book. He would say, "The Bible says it; I believe it; that settles it." He preached it as truth. He proclaimed it as authority. He preached it as he was illuminated by the Holy Spirit. He preached against sin. He told us about the Ten Commandments, the "thou shalt nots" of the Bible.

Today, when the Word of God is neglected or not followed, people develop their own ethical way: "if you feel right about it, it's okay." As a result, we have moral bankruptcy. We have big problems in homes and marriages.

The old-time religion was a religion of the Book. It proclaimed: "I know the Bible is true!"

IT WAS A RELIGION OF THE **BLOOD**.

A scarlet thread runs throughout the Bible from Genesis to the end of Revelation, and that means salvation through the blood. Peter, Philip, Stephen, and Paul proclaimed it.

The modernist denies the blood-stained way. This unbeliever states his position bluntly:
1. If you have tractors, you don't need faith.
2. If you have penicillin, you don't need prayer.
3. If you have positive thinking, you don't need

salvation.
4. If you have a state, you don't need a church.
5. If you have manuals of science, you don't need the Bible.
6. If you have Edison and Einstein, you don't need Jesus.

Yet God says the blood of Jesus redeems us (1 Peter 1:19-20), brings us near (Ephesians 2:13), makes peace (Colossians 1:20), justifies (Romans 5:9), and cleanses (1 John 1:9).

IT WAS A RELIGION OF THE **BREATH OF GOD**.

Old-time people believed in the Holy Spirit, the personal presence and power of God in the lives of those who trust Him. The word translated as "spirit" literally means, in its root word, *breath of God*. The moment a person believes in Jesus Christ as Savior, the breath of God takes residence in his or her life. This means that the breath of God in the person of the Holy Spirit is with us, beside us. Jesus said, *"If I go away, I will send One that shall be like Me, the Paraclete, who will walk beside you."*

The old-time preacher believed in the supernatural presence of God. In the book of Acts, God's presence was seen in the lives of His followers. Today the book of Acts is still being written, for the Holy Spirit dwells in us right now.

IT WAS A RELIGION OF THE **BLESSED HOPE**.

This blessed hope is the second coming of Jesus Christ. Jesus (John 14:3), Paul (Titus 2:13), Peter (2 Peter 3:12), and John (Revelation 22:20) proclaimed it. Likewise, our forefathers believed in the literal, visible appearing of the Lord Jesus Christ the second time. He is coming for His

Church, His people, the redeemed Body of Christ. He is coming as King of Israel, King of nations, King of Kings and Lord of all.

It is called the blessed hope, and what a hope we have! It is the hope for this troubled world. We need to **look up**—the signs of His coming are here (2 Peter 3:9-14). We need to **shape up**—walk honestly, be found faithful and blameless (vs. 14). We need to **speak up**—preach God's judgment against sin and the need for repentance and warn of His return.

IT WAS A RELIGION THAT TALKED ABOUT A **BEAUTIFUL HEAVEN**.

Jesus talked about Heaven in John 14. John on the isle of Patmos has given us glimpses into the heavenly home. When one looks into the hymn books, there are more wonderful hymns about Heaven than any other theme.

What I like about the old-time religion is that it tells how a person can get to Heaven:

Not by works
Not by turning over a new leaf
Not by baptism or the Lord's Supper
Not by the Reformation
Not by being good

The only way to get to Heaven is by trusting Jesus Christ as Savior. Jesus said, *"I am the way."*

Tis the old-time religion...
Makes me love ev'rybody...
It will do when I am dying...
It will take us all to Heaven....
It's good enough for me!

Worthy
1 Thessalonians 2:12

INTRODUCTION

Definition of *worthy*:
1. Possessing worth
2. Having valuable or useful qualities
3. Deserving of respect or honor

WE ARE NOT WORTHY OF GOD'S MERCIES
1. Genesis 25-32 tells the story of how Jacob deceived Esau out of his birthright and blessing.
    Genesis 25:27-34 – Deception begins.
    Genesis 27:1ff – Deception continues.
    Genesis 27:27 – Jacob receives Isaac's blessing.
    Genesis 32:9 – Jacob feared Esau.
    Genesis 32:10 – *"I am not worthy of blessing. I have deceived Esau out of his birthright."*
2. Luke 15:19 – The Prodigal Son: *"I am not worthy to be called thy son."*
3. We are not worthy of God's blessings. We were lost, undone, our righteousness as filthy as rags. (Sinners – not worthy – not deserving. "I am unworthy.")

WE ARE NOT WORTHY TO SERVE HIM

John 1:27 – John bears witness of the coming of Christ – *"I am not the Christ."* – *"I'm not worthy to tie His shoes."*

Matthew 3:11 – *"I'm not worthy to carry His shoes."*

Often we as Christians are asked to serve. (I was called to preach in 1949 and ordained in 1952. I did not feel worthy.)

 A. Some are called as preachers
 B. Some are called as deacons
 C. Some are called to service for Him – teaching, being a committee member, etc.

Like John, we say *"I am not worthy."*

I remind you we are made worthy through Christ.

 A. He imparts righteousness.
 B. He gives strength.
 C. He energizes us.
 D. He gives us boldness.

OUR SUFFERINGS ARE NOT WORTHY TO BE COMPARED TO THE COMING GLORY

See Romans 8:16-18 – Paul suffered. See also 2 Corinthians 11:23-38.

 A. Suffering is real – physical and mental anguish. (We suffer with Him.)
 B. v. 17 – On the other hand, there is glory in suffering that is going to be revealed.
 C. How much we suffer for Christ's sake will be nothing compared to the glory awaiting us. Illustration: a lady in Beaver Dam, Kentucky who was going through intense pain and suffering. She asked me, "Why do I have to suffer?"

My answer to her:

Some suffering is a result of sin (but not all suffering comes because of personal sins).

Suffering that comes our way helps us to understand the suffering Jesus went through.

Suffering is a part of life, that God may be glorified.

There is glory awaiting us through suffering.

OUR WALK IS TO BE A WORTHY WALK

1 Thessalonians 2:11-12 – Your walk should reflect what Christ has done for you.

Ephesians 4:1ff – Walk like Jesus:

Walk humbly
Walk showing a caring spirit
Walk in unity
Walk in peace
Walk with honor
Walk in His love

This is your vocation, your calling as a Christian. Just as Buford Pusser, in *Walking Tall*, walked to defeat the criminal element, we should walk with God against the spiritual forces of evil.

In Genesis, Enoch walked with God and went home to be with the Lord.

GOD IS WORTHY OF OUR PRAISE

Look at Revelation 4:11 – Praise is due Him!

God is worthy → Honor Him

God created us → Glorify Him
God re-created us → Adore Him

CLOSING

Remember:

We are not deserving of God's mercy.

We are not worthy to serve Him.

Our sufferings are not worthy to compare to His coming glory.

Our walk is to be worthy.

God is worthy of praise!

From *The Baptist Hymnal*:

Worthy of Worship

Worthy of worship, worthy of praise,
Worthy of honor and glory,
Worthy of all the glad songs we can sing,
Worthy of all of the off'rings we bring.

Worthy of rev'rence, worthy of praise,
Worthy of love and devotion,
Worthy of bowing and bending of knees,
Worthy of all this, and added to these.

You are worthy, Father, Creator!
You are worthy, Savior, Sustainer!
You are worthy, worthy and wonderful,
Worthy of worship and praise.

God's Toolbox
Psalm 139:1-10

INTRODUCTION

I have preached "The Devil's Toolbox" in the past, referring to the tools that the Devil, our Adversary, is using to lead people astray to destruction.

I believe in a personal Devil. I also believe that the Bible teaches us about a personal God. God is sovereign, almighty, all-powerful, all-knowing, all-seeing. The psalmist bears this out in Psalm 139:

> O Lord, You have searched me and known me.
> You know when I sit down and when I rise up;
> You understand my thoughts from afar.
> You scrutinize my path and my lying down
> And are intimately acquainted with all my ways.
> Even before there is a word on my tongue,
> Behold, O Lord, You know it all.
> You have enclosed me behind and before
> And laid Your hand upon me.
> Such knowledge is too wonderful for me;
> It is too high, I cannot attain it.
> Where can I go from Your Spirit?
> Or where can I flee from Your presence?
> If I ascend to heaven, You are there;
> If I make my bed in Sheol, behold, You are there.
> If I take the wings of the dawn,
> If I dwell in the remotest part of the sea,
> Even there Your hand will lead me
> And Your right hand will lay hold of me.
> – Psalm 139: 1-10

Satan is using his tools. But Psalm 139 is a picture of God dealing with His creation.

1. One cannot run from God.
2. One cannot hide from God.

God uses His tools, too.

TOOL #1: THE BIBLE

1. Leads men to God – shows them the way of life
2. Builds, edifies
3. A lamp unto our feet

Thank God for the Bible!

TOOL #2: THE HYMN BOOK

1. God wants us to praise Him.
2. Psalms are poems of praise to a covenant God.
3. Colossians 3:16 – *Let the word of Christ dwell in you richly in all wisdom, teaching and admonishing one another in psalms and hymns and spiritual songs, singing with grace in your hearts to the Lord.*
4. Singing from the hymn book softens the heart and prepares the way for God's message.

TOOL #3: THE POCKET BOOK

1. All that we have is a gift of God. He is the Owner.
2. We are stewards – managers.

TOOL #4: THE TELEPHONE (PRAYER)

Philippians 4:6 – *Do not be anxious about anything, but in everything, by prayer and petition, with thanksgiving, present your requests to God.*

Romans 8:26 – *In the same way, the Spirit helps us in our weakness. We do not know what we ought to pray for, but the Spirit Himself intercedes for us with groans that words cannot express.*

1 Thessalonians 5:16 – *Be joyful always; pray continually; give thanks in all circumstances, for this is God's will for you in Christ Jesus.*

TOOL #5: THE CHURCH

God's Church is not a building. It is a fellowship of believers.

1. God has chosen His Church as an instrument to carry out His purpose.
2. Each church is a fellowship of love where concern and compassion for each other is shown.
3. Don't neglect this fellowship. Don't neglect this worship. God uses believers to minister to others.

TOOL #6: THE DOVE

This is a symbol of the Holy Spirit.

1. The coming of the Holy Spirit
2. The indwelling of the Holy Spirit
3. The work of the Holy Spirit – convicts, guides, teaches, helps, strengthens

TOOL #7: THE CROSS OF JESUS CHRIST
1. God demonstrated His love.
2. God sent His only begotten Son.
3. Don't neglect the cross, God's instrument of salvation!

CLOSING

Use these tools of God when the Devil tries to use his tools against you:

THE BIBLE

THE HYMN BOOK

THE POCKET BOOK (GIVING/GRATITUDE)

PRAYER

THE CHURCH

THE HOLY SPIRIT

THE CROSS OF CHRIST

The Promise of God in the Rainbow
Genesis 9:8-17

INTRODUCTION

One of the loveliest sights in God's creation is that of the rainbow. A rainbow occurs when rain is falling in one portion of the sky and the sun is shining in another.

Rainbows I have seen in my lifetime: rainbows as a child, rainbows on golf courses, a rainbow on the Sea of Galilee.

There are songs about rainbows that we sing or hear others sing: *Somewhere over the Rainbow*, *He Sends the Rainbow*, *Sunshine with the Rainbow*.

The rainbow after the Flood, in our text, could be labeled the greatest, most beautiful, most meaningful that has ever appeared. The rainbow in our text is a sermon in nature, for it tells us that God will never, under any circumstance, break His word. Never again will the earth be destroyed by water.

Note God's covenant in the text: *I establish My covenant with you: Never again will all life be destroyed by the waters of a flood; never again will there be a flood to destroy the earth* (verse 11).

What is the message of the rainbow in that day and our day?

THE RAINBOW SPEAKS TO US OF THE **POWER** OF GOD.

We are living in a crazy world, a world constantly boasting of its power. I have seen:

- Power engines at Hoover Dam
- The power of the engines that propelled Neil Armstrong into space
- God's great power

God is all-powerful. His power is seen as He produces a rainbow in the clouds.

- When we see it, it tells us what God is like. Psalm 19:1 – *The heavens declare the glory of God; the skies proclaim the work of His hands.*
- It speaks of His greatness and majesty.
- It speaks of His mighty and strong power. Isaiah 40:26 – *Lift up your eyes and look to the heavens: Who created these? He who brings out the starry host one by one and calls forth each of them by name. Because of His great power and mighty strength, not one of them is missing.*
- There is power in the blood!
- There is power in the gospel of Christ! Romans 1:16 – *For I am not ashamed of the gospel of Christ, for it is the power of God for salvation to everyone who believes.*

THE RAINBOW SPEAKS TO US OF THE **PERFECTION** OF GOD.

The rainbow is not only the blending of colors flawlessly, but it is indescribably beautiful and majestic in its splendor.

And if God's handiwork is so perfect, what must God be like Himself?

- Perfect in purity. *Your eyes are too pure to look on evil. You cannot tolerate wrongdoing.* – Habakkuk 1:13
- Perfect in character. *They celebrate Your abundant goodness and joyfully sing of Your righteousness.* – Psalm 145:7
- Perfect in beauty and loveliness. *One thing I ask from the Lord, this only do I seek: that I may dwell in the house of the Lord all the days of my life, to gaze on the beauty of the Lord and to seek Him in His temple.* – Psalm 27:4
- Perfect in graciousness and compassion. *The Lord is gracious and compassionate, slow to anger and rich in love. The Lord is good to all. He has compassion on all He has made.* – Psalm 145:8-9

Yes, He is perfect: holy, righteous, beautiful, and a God of love.

THE RAINBOW SPEAKS TO US OF THE **PROMISES** OF GOD.

Every promise in the Book is mine, every promise in every chapter and verse. Every promise in the Word of God is for us.

Matthew 24:35 – *"Heaven and earth will pass away, but My words will never pass away."*

He will fulfill every promise that He ever made:

- He will complete His Church.
- He will rapture His Church.
- He will establish the throne of David.
- He will overthrow all enemies and exalt the Lord Jesus Christ.
- He will judge the saved and the lost.
- He will save *whosoever* will call on Him.

The promises of God are certain. They are also varied. There is a promise for every need, every circumstance, every situation.

When I was a lad, I was told there was a pot of gold at the end of the rainbow. God's promise is not gold. His promise is to be with us. His promise is Heaven at the end of this life.

THE RAINBOW SPEAKS TO US OF THE **PURPOSE** OF GOD.

God's purpose is two-fold: judgment and grace (verses 13-14).

- The rainbow speaks to us of grace.

- The cloud speaks to us of judgment.

All through human history these two are placed side by side.

Throughout the Bible we read of God's condemnation of man's sin, but also side by side with this we read of His love for sinners and His day of deliverance. God must punish sin, for He is a holy God, and He is altogether righteous. But He loves the sinner and longs for his or her salvation.

- Note in Romans 6:23 the cloud and the bow: *The wages of sin is death, but the gift of God is eternal life through Jesus Christ our Lord.*
- Note in Romans 11:22 the severity of God and the goodness of God: *Consider therefore the kindness and sternness of God: sternness to those who fell, but kindness to you.*
- Note in John 3:39 the cloud for the sinner and the rainbow for the saint. *Whoever believes in the Son has eternal life, but whoever rejects the Son will not see life, for God's wrath remains on them.*
- Note in 1 Peter 4:12-13 the cloud of trials and the rainbow of joy, gladness, and glory revealed. *Dear friends, do not be surprised at the fiery ordeal that has come on you to test you, as though something strange were happening to you. But rejoice inasmuch as you participate in the sufferings of Christ, so that you may be overjoyed when His glory is revealed.*

- Note in 2 Corinthians 12:7-9 the cloud (the thorn in the flesh) and the rainbow (the promise of the all-sufficiency of His grace). *Therefore, in order to keep me from becoming conceited, I was given a thorn in my flesh, a messenger of Satan to torment me. Three times I pleaded with the Lord to take it away from me. But He said to me, "My grace is sufficient for you, for My power is made perfect in weakness." Therefore I will boast all the more gladly about my weaknesses.*

SUMMARY

God's rainbow reminds us of His power, perfection, promise, and purpose.

Blessedness
Numbers 6:24

24 The Lord bless you and keep you.

INTRODUCTION

Bless, blessing, blessed (or *blest*) and *blessedness* are very familiar words to the Christian. They speak of happiness, peace, prosperity, and wellbeing. They have a range of meaning which becomes fuller each time we use them.

There are several words in Hebrew and Greek which are translated *blessedness*, and they express speaking, wishing, and giving good things; praising; being happy; speaking well of others; and honoring.

Tonight, I want to gather all these meanings together by setting forth the following truths.

GOD IS THE SOURCE OF BLESSEDNESS

He is the all-wise and all-giving Creator whose gifts include:

1. Prosperity and peace

2. Life to His creation

3. Care for His people

4. Revealing of Himself in Jesus and His gift of the Holy Spirit.

5. His presence

This prayer of Moses in Numbers 6:24 affirms that blessedness comes from God.

MAN RECEIVES BLESSEDNESS FROM GOD

This is the other side of what we have just noticed. We could make a long list of what we receive as God's blessing.

Psalm 24:5 is an example: *He shall receive a blessing from the Lord and righteousness from the God of his salvation.* All of life's gifts—plenty, peace, success, beauty, wisdom—are from God.

MAN BLESSES MAN

1. Isaac blessed Jacob and his sons.
2. Moses and Joshua blessed the Israelites.
3. Solomon blessed his people, and they in turn blessed him.

This kind of blessing was much more than wishing them good luck. It resulted in power, because it focused on the blessedness which God alone gives.

MAN BLESSES GOD

This is somewhat puzzling to many. If all blessedness is in God and from God, how can man add to this by blessing God? Is this not arrogance? Not when we realize that **blessing God means responding to God** by giving Him praise.

The Psalmist often calls on himself and others to bless the Lord. For example, look at Psalm 103:1 – *Bless the Lord, O my soul! And all that is within me bless His holy name!*

The highest praise man gives is when he blesses God for the gift of the Savior.

Blessed be the God and Father of our Lord Jesus

Christ, who has blessed us in the heavenly realms with every spiritual blessing in Christ. For He chose us in Him before the creation of the world to be holy and blameless in His sight. In love He predestined us for adoption to sonship through Jesus Christ, in accordance with His pleasure and will—to the praise of His glorious grace, which He has freely given us in the One He loves. In Him we have redemption through His blood, the forgiveness of sins, in accordance with the riches of God's grace that He lavished on us. With all wisdom and understanding, He made known to us the mystery of His will according to His good pleasure, which He purposed in Christ, to be put into effect when the times reach their fulfillment—to bring unity to all things in heaven and on earth under Christ. – Ephesians 1:3-10

JESUS SPEAKS IN THE BEATITUDES OF THOSE WHO ARE BLESSED

These are the deprived, the poor, the hungry, the merciful, and the peacemakers. Today the world calls few of these blessed or envies them. But because they share qualities of the Lord Jesus, they share in the fullness of His Kingdom.

BLESSEDNESS IS ASSOCIATED WITH THE COMING OF CHRIST

1. In His earthly ministry.

2. In His exalted power in the future.

The opposite of *bless* is *curse*. Moses speaks of this in Deuteronomy 30:15-20.

[15] *See, I set before you today life and prosperity, death and destruction.*

¹⁶ *For I command you today to love the L̪ᴏʀᴅ your God, to walk in obedience to Him, and to keep His commands, decrees and laws; then you will live and increase, and* **the L̪ᴏʀᴅ your God will bless you** *in the land you are entering to possess.*

¹⁷ *But if your heart turns away and you are not obedient, and if you are drawn away to bow down to other gods and worship them,*

¹⁸ *I declare to you this day that you will certainly be destroyed. You will not live long in the land you are crossing the Jordan to enter and possess.*

¹⁹ *This day I call the heavens and the earth as witnesses against you that* **I have set before you life and death, blessings and curses**. *Now choose life, so that you and your children may live*

²⁰ *and that you may love the L̪ᴏʀᴅ your God, listen to His voice, and hold fast to Him. For the L̪ᴏʀᴅ is your life, and He will give you many years in the land He swore to give to your fathers—Abraham, Isaac, and Jacob.*

God's Goldmines
Ephesians 2:4 – Philippians 4:19
Psalm 104:24 – Romans 10:12

INTRODUCTION

In a daily newspaper there was a news item with this caption over it: "Is There a Goldmine in Your Attic?" The story beneath was very fascinating. It read like this:

An elderly lady was looking in the attic for something she needed. In an old chest drawer she found a faded, yellowed envelope containing some valuable-looking documents. She took them to the bank and was told these were bonds worth about $60,000.

The writer finished the story this way:

There may not be goldmines in your attic at home, but as Russell Cronwell once said, "There are acres of diamonds and gold all around you that have not been discovered. Some may be in your mind and personality."

Today I want to use the Word of God to point out places where there are undiscovered goldmines.

THE FIRST PLACE IS EXPRESSED IN PSALM 104:24 – THE EARTH IS FULL OF RICHES.

- I have been told and have read that mining for gold continues throughout the world: in Alaska, California and other states out west, and countries in Africa.

235

- I also know that there are millions of dollars' worth of gold bars secure and safe at Fort Knox in Kentucky and other places around the world.
- In my travels to the Grand Canyon, Venezuela, the Philippines, Chile, Israel, and Korea—east, west, north, and south—I have seen illustrations of the undiscovered wealth that God has hidden beneath the surface of the earth.
- Yes, God owns the cattle on a thousand hills and also all the gems under the hills!
- We must not forget that this is God's world. He created it. He owns it. He is sovereign over it, and the earth is full of His riches.

THE SECOND UNDISCOVERED NUGGET IS THE GOLDMINE OF HUMANITY.

- God made man in His own image.
- When Adam and Eve sinned in the Garden of Eden, that image was marred, and man lost fellowship with God.
- However, God loved His creation and desired fellowship with humanity, the highest creation.
- This is when God provided His only begotten Son, Jesus, to die on the cross for our sins.
- It is by faith in Jesus Christ that men, women, boys, and girls are brought back into fellowship with God.
- In this way, today, God's highest creation can become a somebody:

--Billy Graham
--Clarence Stewart
--And as I look over the congregation and see you, it reminds me that you are goldmines that have been re-created by God.

THE THIRD GOLDMINE IS THE GOLDMINE OF PRAYER.

- In the words of Jesus, we are promised, *"If you shall ask anything in My name, I will do it."* This is repeated six times in John 14:13-16:23.
    1. Prayer is the most powerful thing in the world.
    2. Prayer can change anything.
    3. Prayer can change a sinner into a saint.
    4. Prayer can provide the strength to conquer a bad habit.
    5. Prayer can wipe from our lives any evil intent.
    6. Prayer can help overcome our biggest obstacles.
    7. Prayer can bring healing when there seems to be no hope.
- Sid Gordon, a devout man of God, wrote: "Prayer is the mightiest thing in human hands. If we know how to pray, nothing is impossible." Yes, prayer is God's goldmine, and His answers are God-given, golden nuggets for us.

- Unfortunately, this is a goldmine from God that many people have never fully discovered.

THE FOURTH HIDDEN NUGGET IS THE GOLDMINE OF INFLUENCE.

- Most of us are too careless or maybe just too thoughtless about our influence.
- Romans 14:7 – *For none of us lives to himself, and no man dies to himself.* We are influencing people away from God, or we are influencing people to get right with Him by following God ourselves.
- The words of a hymn:

    Your life's a book before their eyes;
    They're reading it through and through.
    Say, does it point them to the skies?
    Do others see Jesus in you?

    1. Your influence at home is important.
    2. As you live your life in the workplace, it doesn't go unnoticed.
    3. Our attitude toward our church may be a deciding factor in the salvation of those who know us.
    4. The responsibility of making a church a vital influence in the community lies at the door of the members.
    5. Someone has written this: "Your influence as a church member can help the church to prosper and can

be used by God to touch the life someone who needs Jesus."
6. Yes, your influence can be a goldmine for the cause of Christ.

THE LAST NUGGET IS THE GOLDMINE OF THE GOSPEL.

- Romans 1:16 – *I am proud of the gospel of Christ, for it is the power of God for salvation.*
- The gospel is the power that changes a person's life.
- Philippians 4:19 says, *"God has the power of His riches in glory to save you."*
- Paul says in Ephesians 2:4-5 – *"But God, who is rich in mercy, because of His great love with which He loved us, even when we were dead in trespasses, made us alive together with Christ (by grace you have been saved)."*
- In Romans 10:12 Paul says, *"The same Lord over all is rich unto them that call upon Him."*
- Some years ago I went to Siluria, Alabama to help my friend in a revival meeting. I was getting over my thirty-two radiation treatments for cancer of the throat. We went to visit his brother-in-law who had lung cancer. I shared the gospel with him, and he asked Christ to come into his heart. I discovered again that day that the gospel is an undiscovered goldmine.

SUMMARY

God's Undiscovered Goldmines
the riches of His creation
the wonder of being human, made in His image
the privilege of prayer
the importance of our influence
the power of the gospel

Isn't it time for you to start mining for gold?

Nahum's Message
Nahum 1:7

INTRODUCTION

In the midst of sin and wrongdoing, in a time when evil is running rampant and idolatry and wickedness abound, when things happen we cannot understand, we need to hear and heed Nahum's message. Today let us note three tremendous truths about God from Nahum 1:7.

GOD IS GOOD

The God of creation, the God of the Jew, the God of the Gentile, the God of all people—He is a good God.

- He is trustworthy and dependable. You can count on God when all else fails.
- The story is told of someone, critical of God, crying out, "God is nowhere!" A godly man heard his words and changed them, moving the "w" and adding a space, and exclaimed: "No, God is now here!"
- God has been good to our families. God has been good to our church. God has been good to us as individuals, even when we sin. If we will let Him, God will be good to us in the future. The future is as bright as the promises of God.

- Psalm 34:8 – *Taste and see that the Lord is good. Blessed is the one who takes refuge in Him.*
- Psalm 86:5 – *You, Lord, are forgiving and good, abounding in love to all who call to You.*
- Psalm 23:6 – *Surely goodness and mercy will follow me all the days of my life, and I will dwell in the house of the Lord forever.*

GOD IS A STRONGHOLD IN THE TIME OF TROUBLE

He is a stronghold in the time of need, hurt, pain, trials, and sorrows. Nahum 1:3 – *The Lord is slow to anger but great in power; the Lord will not leave the guilty unpunished. His way is in the whirlwind and the storm, and the clouds are the dust of His feet.*

- God, with all His might, is accessible. Call upon Him. The Psalmist said, *"I sought the Lord."*
- God is like a fortress. He is that Rock of Gibraltar who stands with us.
- In Jamaica, they sang these words:
  Closer than a brother my Jesus is to me.
  He's my dearest Friend in ev'rything I do.
  He's my Rock, my Shield and Hiding Place.
  Closer than a brother Jesus is to me.

GOD PROVIDES SALVATION AND SECURITY

He knows those who trust in Him. He is aware of a person's faith.

- **He saves us.** You don't deserve it. I don't. We, His creations, do not deserve salvation.
- **He secures us.** He knows those who trust in Him. He knows my name and your name. This speaks of the security we have in Christ. Jesus said, *"The sheep hear My voice, and I know them."* Paul says, *"Nothing can separate us from the love of God."* We are saved to the uttermost.
- Hebrews 7:25 – *Therefore He is able to save completely those who come to God through Him, because He always lives to intercede with God on their behalf.*
- Acts 2:21 – *And everyone who calls on the name of the Lord will be saved.*
- John 6:37 – *All those the Father gives Me will come to Me, and whoever comes to Me I will never drive away.*
- Another song from Jamaica:
  He never fails me yet, He never fails me yet;
  Jesus Christ never fails me yet.
  Ev'rywhere I go I want the world to know –
  Jesus Christ never fails me yet.
- **He is the sufficient one.** In our rebellion and guilt, He offers pardon and forgiveness. In our anxiety, He promises peace. In our weakness, He provides strength. When death comes to friends and family, He reminds us of life. God cares for us!
- Psalm 50:15 – *Call on Me in the day of trouble; I will deliver you, and you will honor Me.*

- Isaiah 41:10 – *So do not fear, for I am with you; do not be discouraged, for I am your God. I will strengthen you and help you; I will uphold you with My righteous right hand.*
- Psalm 46:1 – *God is our refuge and strength, an ever-present help in trouble.*

NAHUM'S MESSAGE:

**The Lord is good,
a stronghold in the day of trouble;
He knows those who take refuge in Him.
1:7**

The Greatest Love Story
John 3:11 – 1 John 4:7-11 – Romans 5:8
1 John 4:21 – 1 John 5:2,3 – 1 John 2:13

INTRODUCTION

Ask any number of people you meet what the world needs now, and you would get various responses:
- more Social Security
- the old-time religion
- good moral leadership
- someone to challenge us
- more time off
- people who want to work
- a renewed emphasis on honesty and integrity
- safety in our streets
- peace on earth
- more fun

The list is endless.

From the words of a once popular song: "What the world needs now is love, sweet love." That answer is correct: love is what's needed. Bertrand Russell said, "There is a longing for love today." But what kind of love do we need?

The English word *love* has different meanings. It is often misunderstood. The New Testament was written in the Greek language. The Grecians had four different meanings for love:

1. **Eros** is erotic love, romantic love. Passion is involved.
2. **Philo** or **philia** is the friend type of love, brotherly love. Philadelphia, the City of Brotherly Love, gets its name from this word.
3. **Storge** is family love, such as the love of a parent for a child. A mother's love is *storge*.
4. **Agape**, the greatest love, is God's kind of love. It is love as only God can give. God's love for us in Jesus is *agape*.

From our text in 1 John 4, let us notice some truths about the greatest kind of love – God's love.

GOD'S LOVE IS **EXPRESSED**.

His love is manifested. God took the initiative.

- I remind you that the world is sinful. All have sinned. We are sinners by nature, sinners by choice, sinners by practice.
- Romans 5:8 – *God shows His love for us this way: while we were sinners, Christ died for us.*
- Penetrating the doom of this sin-cursed earth is the fact that God loves us.
- The crowning proof of God's love took place at Calvary. God gave His love; God manifested His love; God expressed His love. John 3:16 – *For God so loved the world that He gave His only begotten Son..."*

- Tradition says that while Christ was hanging on the cross, angels in Heaven came together and said, "We are going to earth and rescue Jesus." God said, "No!" God spared not His Son.
- The day before Calvary, Jesus prayed in the Garden of Gethsemane, "Father, if You can accomplish the redemption of mankind in any other way, do it." There was no other way. God sent His only begotten Son for me and you.
- The gospel hymn says: "Why should He love me so? Why should my Savior to Calvary go?"
- The answer is this: When Adam and Eve sinned in the Garden of Eden, the fellowship with God and His creation was severed and lost. God loved His creation so much that He willingly sent His Son to die for our sins.
- This is the world's greatest love.

GOD'S LOVE IS NOT ONLY EXPRESSED; IT CAN BE **EXPERIENCED**.

1 John 4:9 – *This is how God showed His love among us: He sent His one and only Son into the world **that we might live through Him**.*

1. If I were to ask you to share the greatest experience in your life, some would say:

        -- deer hunting or fishing
        -- a winning touchdown
        -- getting my diploma at graduation
        -- golf
        -- marriage
        -- a new baby

2. All the above are great experiences. But the Scripture indicates and our own hearts know that the greatest experience is when we by faith trust Jesus Christ as our Savior.
3. When we experience God's love in Christ and our sins are forgiven, there is joy in our lives. We feel clean inside, and we have eternal life.

THE THIRD TRUTH IN GOD'S GREATEST LOVE IS THAT, AFTER EXPERIENCING SALVATION, YOU NEED TO **EXERCISE** THE LOVE YOU HAVE FOUND.

     A. By public profession of your faith
     B. By following Christ in baptism
     C. By starting to grow as a disciple of Christ
     D. 1 John 4:11 – *"love others"*
     E. 1 John 4:21 – *"love brothers and sisters in Christ"*
     F. By keeping His commandments
     G. By showing love for the unsaved

Aren't you glad that God's greatest love story included you? Remember: He expressed His love, and now you need to exercise (reflect, show) this love to others always.

My brother Ivan trusted Christ as his Savior. He was ordained as deacon. He was the president of the church's Brotherhood program. He had a beautiful wife and five children. The night before he was killed at Armco in a tragic accident, he told our brother Chuck: "I am going to commit myself to telling more people about Jesus, so they can be saved."

After Ivan's funeral, Chuck and I were talking about his commitment to win others to Christ. That day we made a covenant do just that, to fulfill the Great Commission. We decided to exercise the love that we have found in Christ.

The Excitement of Going to Church
(The Joy of Worship)
John 20:19-25

INTRODUCTION

A young couple moved into a community in Pulaski. They had no friends who went to church on Sunday, and they needed some guidance as to where they should go. So they looked next-door for help. Their neighbors were David and Eileen Dale. As David and Eileen left their home to attend our Baptist church, the couple watched them get into their car and, even though they didn't know them, decided to follow them to First Baptist Church. Later they moved their membership here.

Sometime later I asked them about this. Their response was, "We always had a habit of going to church. The joy of worshiping God in church was important to us."

This is not the case with some people, even Christians. Going to church is drudgery to some folks. There seems to be no spiritual hunger to meet Jesus in the worship experience.

I believe if we really love the Lord, we should find our churchgoing a joyous experience. Going to church does not make one a Christian, but a Christian will want to go to church. He or she will want to gather with the Lord's people on the Lord's Day and have a happy experience in worship. For sure, there are some of God's people who are not free to go to the Lord's house on His day, due to circumstances such as sickness, age, infirmity, or legitimate duties connected with the home or with their work. For everyone else, the joy of worship in the Lord's house should be an exciting experience.

What are the characteristics of the gathering of the Lord's people, and what lessons should we learn from John 20:19-25?

A DAY WE HALLOW THE LORD'S RESURRECTION

Verse 19 – They met together on the same day, being the first day of the week. It was not the seventh day, not the Jewish Sabbath, but it was the Lord's Day. The seventh day, Sabbath, which was the memorial of Creation, was now replaced by the first day of the week, the day on which Jesus rose again. Thus Sunday to us is the memorial of the New Creation. From that time to this, Christians have hallowed the first day of the week as the Lord's Day, and they have met on that day for worship and service.

--The Lord's Day was foreshadowed in the Feast of First Fruits (Leviticus 23:15-16). This feast typified the Lord's resurrection.

--It was on the first day that the Holy Spirit descended to constitute the Church (Acts 2:1-4).

--It was on the first day of the week that early Christians met for worship and to present their offering to the Lord (1 Corinthians 16:2).

A DAY WE HAVE AN APPOINTMENT TO KEEP

Verse 19 – When the door was closed, the disciples were assembled. It was shut in fear, for Jesus had been killed. They were being cautious. In other words, they had an appointment to assemble before the door was closed.

Every time we go to worship on the first day of the week, we are keeping an appointment with the Lord. We should not be careless about our appointment with the Lord.

One cannot be careless about his or her job. One goes to work whether it is wet, hot, or cold. We must not be careless about our worship with the Lord.

A DAY WE MEET JESUS

Verse 19 – Jesus came and stood in their midst.

It is true that we meet members of the church, our family. But the thing that is first and foremost is that we meet Jesus, our beloved Lord. *"For where two or three are gathered together in My name, I am in the midst of them"* (Matthew 18:20).

It is this which makes every time of worship so precious, so wonderful, so unique, so helpful. It is not the presence of the preacher, of the crowd, or the attractiveness of the building. It is the person of the Lord who is in our midst. What joy there is when we worship and adore Him!

A DAY WE RECEIVE

--**The comfort of His Word** (verses 19-22) – "He said" or "He saith…"

--**The awareness of His voice** – He speaks to us when we worship. All week we listen to other voices, to many voices. Now we come to listen to our Savior. *"I will hear what the Lord has to speak"* (Psalm 85:8). He speaks to us through music, prayers, and from His Word.

--**The assurance of His love** (verse 20) – When Jesus had shown them His hands and side, they knew that out of love for them He paid the price for their sins. *"If we walk in the light as He is in the light, we have fellowship with one another* (1 John 1:7).

--**The gift of His peace** (verse 24) – Jesus said, *"Peace be with you."* In John 14:7 He said, *"Peace I leave with you."* Ephesians 2:14 says, *"He is our peace."* In a world filled with trouble and chaos, it is good to come into His presence and feel peace. As the song says, "Peace, peace, wonderful peace, coming down from the Father above...."

--**The knowledge of His will** (verse 21) – While they were with Him, the Lord had something to say to them about their responsibility toward those who did not know Him. *"As My Father has sent Me, so send I you."* This is His will for us. We are to go throughout this area and declare to all people that if they believe on the Lord Jesus Christ, their sins can be forgiven.

--**The blessing of His presence and the power of His Holy Spirit** (verse 25) – It is impossible to tell others of the Savior and to do this in our own strength, and so our Lord said to them, as He says to us, *"Receive the Holy Spirit."* As we meet in the Lord's presence, we are reminded that the Holy Spirit's presence is with us, and He equips us for His service.

These are some of the blessings we receive when we go to church in the right spirit and with a longing to meet Jesus.

In closing, look at verse 23. Those who responded in faith to the Christ who forgives sin would have their sins forgiven. Those who refused

Him would remain in their sin. The believers had the authority to pronounce this message of forgiveness. Their sins had already been forgiven. God makes forgiveness possible in Jesus Christ. All Christians have the authority to proclaim this message.

CLOSING

Starting today and every Sunday ahead, will you commit to true worship?

HALLOW THE LORD'S RESURRECTION BY COMING TO WORSHIP ON THE FIRST DAY.

FAITHFULLY KEEP YOUR APPOINTMENT TO ENTER HIS HOUSE TO WORSHIP.

EXPECT TO MEET JESUS CHRIST AS YOU WORSHIP WITH OTHER BELIEVERS.

GRATEFULLY RECEIVE SPIRITUAL BLESSINGS FROM GOD AS YOU WORSHIP.

Eutychus: Sleeping in the Church
Acts 20:1-12

INTRODUCTION

This is the first record we have of a man who slept at church. He has had many successors. I recall a few years ago when my young son Scott fell asleep at church. My wife and I came home in separate cars, each thinking that the other had carried Scott. When we discovered that he had been left at church, Randy and I hurried back there. We found him still asleep on the pew!

But this morning I want to talk about others who are sleeping.

THERE ARE MANY WHO ARE ASLEEP TO GREAT OPPORTUNITIES FOR CHRISTIAN SERVICE AND THE PERFORMANCE OF CHRISTIAN DUTY.

- Too many are merely spectators. They sit or stand and watch others do the work they should be doing. They miss the joy of working for Christ in His church. Someone said, "A sleeping soldier at the battlefront may be armed with the latest weapons, but if he is asleep, he is good for absolutely nothing to the army and the cause."

- How we need to be awake to our opportunities for service! These include teaching, visiting, calling others, working in VBS, serving on the hospitality committee, serving as usher, working with a group to clean up the church.

THERE ARE THOSE WHO ARE ASLEEP TO THE OPPORTUNITIES OF FRIENDSHIP AND JOY IN GOD'S HOUSE.

- I believe the best people in the world meet right here at Station Camp Baptist Church. In the church you meet with members from different backgrounds and form genuine friendships.
- I met my wife in church.
- One person said to me, "I do not want to miss a church service. I might miss a spiritual blessing."
- The fellowship time at Station Camp Baptist Church is a great time for the congregation – singing, shaking hands, hugging, greeting one another. Truly, we can sing, "Blest be the tie that binds our hearts in Christian love."

THERE ARE MANY WHO ARE ASLEEP TO SINFUL HABITS AND EVIL LIVES.

- This is often something that exists with those who are Christians. The Devil is active in influencing church members to sin.
- The call from the Word of God and from the preacher reminds Christians not to fall into sin. However, many are often asleep to this call to be right with God.
- Every now and then you hear about a person who has fallen into sin, and yet that person is often in church. He or she listens with apparent interest in the sermon, but the heart rejects the truth. How do you account for the downfall? That person was spiritually asleep.

- Jonah slept as he disobeyed God. Demas was asleep. Satan has no worry about one who is asleep.

THERE ARE MANY WHO ARE ASLEEP TO GOD AND ETERNAL LIFE.

- It is quite possible to listen to the preaching of the gospel, calling for repentance and faith and pointing out the eternal loss of the soul, and yet both the will and conscience be asleep.

- Often the preaching from the pulpit is followed by sermons experienced in people's lives—sickness, death, peril, affliction, tragedy. All these remind them: "Hear what the preacher is saying!" But they remain asleep. They have fallen into slumber to God and eternal life.

THERE ARE MANY WHO ARE ASLEEP TO WORSHIP.

- Acts 20 gives us the most illuminating account of early Christian worship. They were celebrating the Resurrection by meeting on the first day of the week. They were breaking bread, observing the Lord's Supper. They listened to a sermon.

- Paul was on his way to Jerusalem, returning from his third missionary journey. He had been to Greece. He had crossed over from Macedonia to Troas. (Perhaps he had a seven-day revival meeting there.) Paul's presence brought a large crowd to the service.

- The service was held in the home of Carpus. It was a large house of three stories. There was no organ, piano, altar, choir, or stained-glass windows, just the plain assembly of the people and the Word of God. In the room many lamps were burning.

- The central figure is Paul. There is no record of his sermon. We can be sure he preached Christ and exhorted them to godly living. That night Paul preached a <u>long</u> sermon, continuing until midnight. The clock had not yet been put on religious services as it is today.

- Perched high up in the window was a young man named Eutychus. This was a dangerous seat, but he could hear and see everything that took place.

- As Paul was preaching, the young man went to sleep and fell out of the window, a three-story fall. This must have horrified the congregation.

- Paul, as always, was a man for emergencies. He took over, restoring the boy to life. Then he resumed his interrupted sermon.

- That young man was asleep to the worship going on around him, just like so many of us today. Like him, we need to be awakened so that we can once again hear the message from God's Word.

CLOSING

To those who may be asleep to opportunities of service and friendship, to those asleep to sin and evil habits, to those who are asleep to God and eternal life, and to those who are asleep to worship, let me close with the Scripture:

Besides this, knowing the time, it is already the hour for you to wake up, for now our salvation is nearer than when we first believed. The night is already over, and the daylight is near, so let us discard the deeds of darkness and put on the armor of light.
–Romans 13:11-12

Awake to righteousness and sin not!
–1 Corinthians 15:34

For what makes everything clear is light. Therefore it is said, "Get up, sleeper, and rise up from the dead, and the Messiah will shine on you." –Ephesians 5:14

Special Occasions

A Father Role Model
Luke 15: 11-32

INTRODUCTION

Father's Day, 2008. For many it is a time for new ties, long-distance calls, Hallmark cards, and family meals. Mother's Day and Father's Day are not good times to eat at a restaurant. The waiting period is just too long.

I do not remember my father. He died before I was two years old. Pauline Stewart, my mother, was both my dad and mom.

Someone has written, "Boys and dads go through stages in life in their relationships."

- At age four we exclaim, "My dad can do anything!"
- At age seven we say, "My dad knows a lot."
- At age twelve we're saying, "Oh well, we can't expect Dad to know everything."
- At age fourteen we say, "My dad is hopelessly out of date and old-fashioned."
- By the time we reach twenty-one years of age we are saying, "What should I expect? He just doesn't understand."
- At age twenty-five we begin to say, "My dad knows a little bit but not too much."
- By the age of thirty we say, "I need to find out what Dad thinks."
- At age forty we ask, "What would Dad have thought?"

- By the time we reach fifty we're saying, "My dad knew everything."
- And at the age of sixty we usually say, "I wish I could talk it over with Dad just one more time."

There are a lot of father role models around today. However, there's one tucked away in the parables of our Lord who is overlooked because he gives away center stage to his two sons. He is the father in the story of the prodigal son and the older brother. There is so much we can learn from him on this Father's Day. He parented his sons with <u>openness</u>.

WE SEE HIM WITH AN OPEN HAND SAYING, "I **RELEASE** YOU."

Read Luke 15:11-13.

- He lets him go—a tough love. Here is a dad who is wise enough to know that what he puts in his child at a young age determines what he becomes later. This father in Luke 15 obviously was an example in the home and gave his sons some standards and absolutes. These standards and absolutes were the very things from which the youngest son chose to rebel.
- Dads should not only be **material** providers, as important as that is. Nor should they be only **mental** providers, as vital as that is. They should be **moral** providers.
- The father in our story opens his hand to his boy and lets him go when the time comes. He didn't have to do this. He could have refused and held back the inheritance.

- There are times when a dad knows what is best but still lets his child go. This father could have denied the son's request. He could have blackmailed his son with the inheritance, saying, "If you leave, you will have no inheritance." He could have done like parents today and played the comparison: "Why can't you be like your big brother? Are you trying to break your mother's heart?"

- Here's a dad who was prepared to stand by what he'd put in his boy from childhood. Solomon, in Proverbs 22:6, says, *"Train up a child in the way he should go, and when he is old he will not depart from it."* Some parents hold kids so tightly they actually end up losing them. But this father let go of his child, saying in essence: "Son, I trust you, but I fear your judgments." Though he was concerned, he did not send a servant to spy on him. As much as his heart was breaking, as much as he knew wrong decisions were ahead, we see the father opening his hand: "Take your inheritance. I release you."

- Yes, he let him go, but he never gave up on him. No matter how dedicated a home may be, there are seasons of disappointment which come our way.

- The boy left home to be free but unfortunately became a slave. Read verses 13-14. The Bible tells us, *"When he had spent all, there arose a famine in the land, and he began to be in want."* Verses 15-16 tell what happened when all was gone. How many times does this happen when one gets outside the umbrella of authority which God has placed over us? Note in verse 17 that a beautiful thing happens in the story: *"He came to himself."* All the years, those years of training, had paid off. He said to himself, "This is not for me. I've been taught better than this."

- I can see the father now, looking down the road. He never gives up. He is a model for this Father's Day because we see him, first of all, with an open hand. He was wise enough to know that the way to keep his son was to let him go, and the way to lose him was to hold him tight.

WE SEE THE FATHER WITH OPEN ARMS SAYING, "I **RECEIVE** YOU."

Read Luke 15:20-24.

- We know the story well. The boy came to himself and started walking toward home. The father came running to receive him.

- The son begins his speech but never gets to give it. The father is full of forgiveness. He had compassion. He forgave him.

- Here was a boy who showed true repentance:

    --He regretted what he had done.

    --He took the blame for his action.

    --He said, *"I have sinned. I have no right to be called your son."*

    --He had a change of attitude and of action.

- The father said, "Let's have a celebration!"

- What a beautiful picture we have of this loving father! We see him with open arms, receiving his son.

- Here we see a beautiful picture of our Heavenly Father. How thankful we are that God does not deal with us according to our sin but according to His tender mercies when we come home to Him in genuine repentance! Look again at the model father. We see him with open hands: "I release you." We see him with open arms: "I receive you."

WE SEE HIM WITH AN OPEN HEART SAYING, "I RESPECT YOU."

Read Luke 15:25-32.

- The most notable characteristic of this dad was his presence. He was there for his boys.

- No matter what the problems of either seemed to be, he was there for them.

- He showed his sons respect and opened his heart to them.

- He paid attention to his eldest son.

- Once the party began to celebrate the return of the prodigal boy, the older brother became angry and would not go in for the party.

- The dad came out, heard his complaint, and opened his heart to assure him of three important things:

    --his abiding presence: *"Son, you are always with me"* – verse 31.

    --his loving provision: *"All I have is yours"* – verse 31.

    --his saving purpose: *"Your brother was dead spiritually and is alive again; he was lost but now is found"* – verse 32.

- We don't know the rest of the story, what the elder son decided to do after the father's speech.

CLOSING

Here was a dad who opened his hand, his arms, and his heart, and he blessed his boys with his presence.

There are sons and daughters in all walks of life who have never had a dad with an open hand, arm, and heart.

But the good news is that our Lord said, *"I will be your Father; you will be my sons and daughters"* – 2 Corinthians 6:18.

- He lets us go, but He never gives up on us.
- When we come to ourselves, He is the loving Heavenly Father who forgives us.
- He was willing to go to Calvary and die on a cross for our sins.
- He who knew no sin became sin for us that we might be forgiven.
- We do not know if the elder son went into the party or not.
- But we do know a loving Father opens Himself—by dying for us. He asks us to come into His banquet celebration. What will *we* do?

The Fabulous Father
Matthew 7:7-11

INTRODUCTION

A popular TV series several years ago was called *Father Knows Best*. Robert Young and Jane Wyatt played the role of parents with three lively and interesting children. Aside from the entertainment, the weekly series revolved around the father. It shared the joys and sorrows of fatherhood. It showed the aspirations and disappointments and the victories of being a father. The program portrayed a father in a folksy, personable manner.

THE BIBLE GIVES US THE PICTURE OF GOD AS A FATHER

1. It is a prominent picture in both the Old and New Testaments:

    a. Jesus taught the disciples to pray, "*Our Father which art in Heaven...*"

    b. In the Sermon on the Mount, Jesus taught His followers to think of God as the Heavenly Father (Matthew 7:11).

2. The picture of God in the Bible is of One who possesses the name and heart of a father.

3. When we think of God as a Father, we do not shiver in fear. Instead, we rest in His love and look into the Bible for greater insight into "our Father which art in Heaven."

A FATHER KNOWS HIS CHILDREN

Think for a moment about an earthly father. Most fathers know the names of all their children, also their birthdays. A good earthly father knows more about his children than mere identity.

    a. He knows particular traits and qualities.

    b. A father knows that one son has a fiery temper and the other son keeps his feelings inward.

    c. A father knows one child's tendency to rebel as well as the other's tendency to obey but inwardly hate obedience.

    d. An earthly father knows the distinctive traits and tendencies of his children.

How much more does the Heavenly Father know His children!

    a. God knows each individual who lives, has lived, and will live.

    b. God has knowledge about each person. He knows us. He knows our names.

    c. He knows our sorrows. He knows our aspirations and our failures. To be sure, the Heavenly Father knows best.

God is above us, beyond us, and different from us. Yet He draws near to us. He wishes to help and be our companion. He is quieting, loving, gracious, merciful, patient, forgiving, and trustworthy.

Illustration: At a convention, a father told me how interested and involved he is in his boy's life. Our Heavenly Father is far more interested in us.

A FATHER HEARS HIS CHILDREN

Look closely at the picture of God as Heavenly Father:

- A godly earthly father takes time to listen to his children.

  a. Yearns to hear the first sounds and words.

  b. Listens as he or she begins to formulate sentences.

  c. Listens to imaginative conversations.

  d. Listens to the rapping of teenagers.

  e. Listens to his children when they are high school and "sophisticated" college students.

- All through his lifetime a father is a listener. Think about the importance of an earthly father taking time to listen to his children. It demonstrates attentiveness, an attempt to understand the children.

- I read about one pediatrician who teaches parents to listen with understanding to their own baby's cries.

  a. One cry could be detected as a hunger call.

  b. One cry could be detected as the attention-getting call.

  c. Then another cry could be from illness.

  Parents need to understand their children's needs by the way they cry.

- Think how much more God understands us. He knows why we ask. He knows what we need. No one understands us or our cries as our Heavenly Father does.

A FATHER CORRECTS HIS CHILDREN

- Look closer into the traits and qualities of an earthly father. When you do a close investigation of a good father, you will inevitably see the quality of discipline. Good fathers rear their children with discipline. It helps the child grow into the authentic best self.

- No good father exercises punishment to harm the child.

- The good father does not discipline the child out of his own frustrations. He does not take out his own inner hostilities on the child.

- Instead, the earthly father disciplines children for their betterment. It breaks them of bad habits and helps them to form good habits. It frees them from harmful traits of character and forms helpful qualities of life.

- Because the father knows what is best for the child, he subjects the child to correction.

- The Heavenly Father corrects. God corrects His children.

    Proverbs 3:12 – *For whom the Lord loves, He corrects, even as a father corrects the son in whom he delights.*

    Deuteronomy 8:5 – *Just as a man chastens his son, so the Lord thy God chastens you.*

    Psalm 94:12 – *Blessed is the man whom You chasten, O Lord, and teach* *him out of Your law.*

Hebrews 12:5-6 – *My son, do not regard lightly the discipline of the Lord, nor be weary when reproved by Him. For the Lord disciplines the one He loves and chastises every son whom He receives.*

- God corrects in love.

God corrects His children for the interest of the entire family.

God corrects to protect the family name.

A FATHER MEETS HIS CHILDREN'S NEEDS

- Any good father will meet the needs of his children.

  a. physical needs – food, clothing, shelter

  b. mental and emotional needs

- God the Father provides for the needs of His children.

  a. During Israel's exodus from Egypt and journey in the wilderness, God provided for their needs.

  b. Psalm 23 – *The Lord is my Shepherd. I shall not want.*

- God cares for His children. But He is not a glorified Santa Claus, giving us what we want. Instead, He gives us what we need: sin-cleansing, salvation, sanctification, Spirit-filling, serenity, sustenance, and so much more!

Reflections on Mothers
(selected notes from two sermons)

REFLECTIONS OF FAMOUS PEOPLE

- Martin Luther: "There is nothing sweeter than the heart of a pious mother."
- George Washington: "My mother taught me Biblical ideas."
- John Quincy Adams: "All that I am my mother made me."
- John Wesley: "My mother was the source from which I derived the guiding principles of my life."
- Dwight L. Moody: "All that is good in my life has come from my mother."

RFLECTIONS FROM MY PERSONAL LIFE

My mother-in-law Lucy Blevins, Mary Lou's mother, is ninety-six years old. She is in Westmoreland Care Center. I have looked through her Bible on several occasions. Recently I looked at remarks written there and Scripture underlined. These reveal her love for the Word of God, and they are a reflection of the qualities she possesses:

- She was a believing mother.
- She was a praying mother.
- She was a witnessing mother.
- She was a singing mother.
- She was a Bible-reading mother.
- She was a trusting and caring mother.
- She was an eternal-hoping mother.

REFLECTIONS ON YOUR OWN MOTHER

The best mother today is your mother. She may have faults, just like you, but she is your mother. She brought you into the world. She taught you. She clothed and fed you.

I believe most Christian mothers of yesterday and today would say, "Do not praise me. Give praise to my Savior." We should not place mothers above everything and merely say sentimental things about them. As we praise them, we should praise their Savior as well.

REFLECTIONS ON YOU AS A MOTHER

A Mother's Day essay by a small boy said, "My mother keeps on speaking terms with God and on spanking terms with me."

Your task as a mother is this and so much more:

- You must set an example.
- You must teach true values.
- You must demonstrate love.
- You must introduce Christ.
- You must involve your child in church.
- You must read Scripture to your child.
- You must pray with your child.

REFLECTIONS FROM THE BIBLE

Noted Bible mothers:

- **Sarah**, barren for years, mother of Isaac
- **Hannah**, a praying mother who promised God, if He gave her a son, that she would give him back to the Lord

- **Elizabeth**, the mother of John the Baptist
- **Mary**, the mother of Jesus
- **Eunice**, the mother of Timothy

PROVERBS 31:10-31

A wife of noble character who can find?
She is worth far more than rubies.
Her husband has full confidence in her
and lacks nothing of value.

She brings him good, not harm,
all the days of her life.
She selects wool and flax
and works with eager hands.

She is like the merchant ships,
bringing her food from afar.
She gets up while it is still night;
she provides food for her family
and portions for her female servants.

She considers a field and buys it;
out of her earnings she plants a vineyard.
She sets about her work vigorously;
her arms are strong for her tasks.

She sees that her trading is profitable,
and her lamp does not go out at night.
In her hand she holds the distaff
and grasps the spindle with her fingers.

She opens her arms to the poor
and extends her hands to the needy.
When it snows, she has no fear for her household;
for all of them are clothed in scarlet.

> She makes coverings for her bed;
> she is clothed in fine linen and purple.
> Her husband is respected at the city gate,
> where he takes his seat among the elders of the land.
>
> She makes linen garments and sells them
> and supplies the merchants with sashes.
> She is clothed with strength and dignity;
> she can laugh at the days to come.
>
> She speaks with wisdom,
> and faithful instruction is on her tongue.
> She watches over the affairs of her household
> and does not eat the bread of idleness.
>
> Her children arise and call her blessed;
> her husband also, and he praises her:
> "Many women do noble things,
> but you surpass them all."
>
> Charm is deceptive, and beauty is fleeting;
> but a woman who fears the Lord is to be praised.
> Honor her for all that her hands have done,
> and let her works bring her praise at the city gate.

Looking Back and Ahead
2 Corinthians 5:11-19

INTRODUCTION

It is time to evaluate the past. Recently I heard of a businessman who said, "I hate the end of the year." When asked why, he replied, "In our business we have to take inventory at the end of the year." He went on to say, "It is a long, tiring process when we check the mistakes and the progress we have made in the business."

If a business needs to take inventory, wouldn't it be a good thing for Christians to evaluate the past year as we come to the final days of 2008? We need to take a look backwards. As we do this...

>...we may recognize those mistakes we have made that have caused us a lot of misery.
>
>...we also may recognize the things we didn't do; we left them undone.
>
>...it may discourage us as we look back and see our failures.

A pastor in a large Atlanta church, in a worship service at the end of the year, asked the members to make a list of the sins, the mistakes, and the wrongs committed during the past year. After he had preached a sermon, he told them, "You can start right now." Then, as soft music was playing, the members went forward to the altar, and each person dropped a folded piece of paper into burning urns. Some stopped to pray before returning to their seats. Written down on the burning papers were the darkest thoughts, the troubling worries, and the deepest hatred that had come to the members' memories during the service. It was a way to forget the past and face the future by symbolically consigning hates and fears to the flaming urns.

Actually, this service of burning thoughts was designed to dramatize God's altar of mercy, where all of our mistakes and our heartaches can be dropped like a shabby old coat and never be put on again.

This is an experience for all of us, for in our walk along the journey of life we must consider:

To leave the old with a burst of song,
To recall the right and forget the wrong,
To forget the thing that binds us fast
To the vain regrets of the year that's past;
To have the strength to let go our hold
Of the not worthwhile of the days grown old.

Now we can forget the things of the past and press on to something new. Having evaluated the past, let us consider the New Year ahead. In just three days 2008 will be history, and we will embark on year 2009. Ahead for us in the New Year will be 12 months, 52 weeks, 365 days, 8760 hours, 525,600 minutes, and 31,536,000 seconds. What will the New Year hold for us?

As we anticipate the next twelve months, it is a good time to focus, to take a fresh look at our life in Christ. The apostle Paul, in the text in 2 Corinthians, states, *"Therefore if any person be in Christ, he is a new creature or creation. The old is gone. The new has come.* "In Christ" is one of Paul's favorite phrases. It stands in contrast to Ecclesiastes chapters one and two, which says, "I have seen everything, I've tried everything, I've done everything, and there is nothing new." Today, as we approach the New Year, let us ask what we have *in Christ*.

IN CHRIST WE HAVE A NEW NATURE.

Before salvation, our nature is sinful. We have what the Bible calls *Adam's sinful nature*. We were once following the path led by Satan. But since we by faith have trusted Jesus, things have changed *in Christ*.

> ...Once we were Christ's enemies; now we are His friends.

> ...Once we were aliens without a home; now we are citizens bound for Heaven.

> ...Once we were rebels, resisting and disobeying Him; now He reigns in our hearts.

IN CHRIST WE HAVE A NEW RELATIONSHIP WITH GOD.

He is our Heavenly Father. The day we become *in Christ*, we become the Heavenly Father's sons and daughters (John 1:12). Galatians 3:26 – *"For you are the children of God."* This new relationship with God leads us to have a new relationship with people, for now we see people through the eyes of Christ.

IN CHRIST WE SHOULD HAVE A NEW SET OF VALUES AND A NEW STANDARD OF BEHAVIOR.

It's easy to become cynical about anybody changing his or her behavior. However, the basis and power to change comes through Christ. When Christ comes in, life changes. We have new values, new standards, new loyalties. This was true of Paul.

It was true of Augustine. It was true of Charles Haddon Spurgeon. They were all changed.

IN CHRIST WE HAVE A NEW REASON FOR LIVING.

Before Christ comes in, we are just existing, keeping up with the Joneses. *In Christ*, life takes on new meaning and purpose. When He comes into one's life, it takes on a divine dimension.

IN CHRIST WE HAVE A NEW RESPONSIBILITY FOR OTHERS.

Verse 19 says that *God was in Christ reconciling the world unto Himself,* and He has committed to us (we who are *in Christ*) the need to share the message with others. We are His ambassadors to people locally and around the world who are without Christ.

IN CHRIST WE HAVE RESTFULNESS OR PEACE ABOUT THE LIFE TO COME.

Jesus' words in the book of Revelation assure us: *"I am the One who makes all things new"* (21:5). There is a new experience coming when time shall be no more, when we no longer will fight the clock and fight the calendar. We will move into eternal life with Christ, and our destiny will be secure, because—*in Christ*—our destiny in His hands.

This morning we have evaluated the past and have anticipated the future. All is new! God, grant that the newness we have *in Christ* will challenge us to face 2009 with joy and expectancy and will lead us to a deeper commitment to Jesus Christ.

Walking in the Light
1 John 1:1-9 – John 8:12

INTRODUCTION

The old year is behind us. The New Year is here. We have begun our walk in 2009. In this year, would you rather walk in darkness or in light? Would you rather walk in total darkness, being blind, or in the light of full vision by which you see and enjoy the beauties and wonders of God's world?

The contrast between darkness and light is one that all of us, I am sure, fully appreciate, at least in a physical sense. The choice between darkness and light in most cases is not difficult to make. We choose light over darkness almost every time. But the choice is not so simple and easy when it comes to spiritual light as opposed to spiritual darkness.

Jesus, however, says we must make that choice. We must choose whether our *"whole body will be full of light"* or full of darkness. We must choose whether we walk in the darkness of this evil world or walk in the light.

NOTE THE **CLAIM** OF THE LIGHT

John 8:12 – *"I am the Light of the World. He who follows Me will not walk in darkness but will have the light of life."*

No other person ever made such a claim as this—not prophet, priest, king, religious teacher, statesman, or poet. Christ is the Light. He is the Light of the World, the Light of lights, the Light of eternity. No one but the Son of God Himself, the

Lord of glory, could say, *"I am the Light of the World."* As the hymn says, "The Light of the World is Jesus!"

The word that Jesus uses is the noun for *light*. The verb in the Greek means *to give light*. In the real and spiritual sense, it refers to the saving truth embodied in Christ, who by His love and influence imparts light to mankind. This light of divine truth includes wisdom, holiness, love, grace, life, and salvation.

Jesus is the Light of life for all His followers. He is the Light for all the needs of life and for all the problems and difficulties. His teachings are words of life. His example is the way of life. Jesus is the Light of the World—of the universe, of nations, peoples, tribes, tongues, and races. He is the Light of government. He is the Light that never fails. In Jamaica, they sing these words:

> He never fails me yet.
> He never fails me yet.
> Jesus Christ never fails me yet.

NOTE THE **COMMAND** TO FOLLOW THE LIGHT

Jesus spoke of believing in the light and walking in the light.

Paul said, *"The night is far gone; the day is at hand. Let us cast off the works of darkness and put on the armor of light"* (Romans 13:12-14).

The nature of darkness is clear. Any kind of evil we do, in thought or word or deed, is darkness. The kingdom of Satan is darkness—hatred, lust, drunkenness, anger. Every kind of evil is darkness.

Far different is the life of the children of God. Christians are those who come to the light, believe the light, and walk in the light. Christians are salt and light, and they walk as children of light.

NOTE THE **COMPANIONSHIP** IN THE LIGHT

We have fellowship with Christ (verse 7).

We have fellowship with one another.

Ephesians 5:8 – *Once you were in darkness, but now you are in the light of the Lord. Walk as children of light.*

The blessed results of this companionship with the living Lord:

--We have the light of life.
--We have light for personal problems and perplexities.
--We know who we are.
--We know where we go from here (Heaven).

NOTE THE **CLEANSING** FROM THE LIGHT

This is the gospel: the precious blood of Jesus saves and cleanses us from all sin.

--It frees us from the **penalty** of sin (death).

--It cleanses us from the **pollution** of sin (the bondage of corruption and wrong in all our lives).

--It delivers us from the very **presence** of sin. (In Heaven, there is no sin, no darkness, no death, no night.)

Reflections on the Lord's Supper
Matthew 26:17-30 – 1 Corinthians 11:23-32

INTRODUCTION

The Lord's Supper has been a central act in the worship of the Church from the very beginning. It was a part of the order of worship before either Scripture reading or preaching.

The Lord's Supper has various meanings. It symbolizes the whole concrete reality of the Church's existence.

This morning, as we prepare to observe Communion once more, I want to share with you, simply and briefly, some thoughtful reflections about this act of worship, which we so often do without thought. We take it without any attempt to understand it and, as a result, without any spiritual depth or meaning.

THE FIRST WORD THAT COMES TO MY MIND WHEN I THINK OF THE LORD'S SUPPER IS **REMEMBRANCE**.

The fellowship around His table has always been, first and foremost, an occasion for recalling to memory the person of Jesus Christ.

As they were eating, Jesus took bread, blessed and broke it, gave it to the disciples and said, "Drink from it, all of you. For this is My blood that establishes the covenant; it is shed for many for the forgiveness of sins." –Matthew 26:26-28

For I received from the Lord what I also passed on to you: on the night when He was betrayed, the Lord Jesus took bread, gave thanks,

broke it, and said, "This is My body which is broken for you. Do this in remembrance of Me." In the same way He also took the cup, after supper, and said, "This cup is the new covenant in My blood. Do this, as often as you drink it, in remembrance of Me."
                                  –1 Corinthians 11:23-26

WHEN I THINK OF THE LORD'S SUPPER, I THINK OF **THANKSGIVING**.

Our Communion service is basically Christ's adaptation of the Jewish Passover feast. The Passover is a religious celebration of thanksgiving that commemorates the deliverance of God's people from their Egyptian taskmasters. The Lord's Supper expresses our gratitude to God for our redemption and deliverance through Christ from the bondage and consequences of sin.

When our Lord took the bread and cup, He gave thanks, and so should we give thanks...

- Thanks for sins that are forgiven and a life that is redeemed.
- Thanks for Jesus Christ—the Way, the Truth, and the Life.
- Grateful for His incarnation and resurrection.
- Grateful for His teachings, preserved for us in the Bible.
- Grateful for His witness that is stirred by the Holy Spirit in our lives.
- Thankful for His constant presence and His abiding companionship.
- Thankful for the victory He gave us.
- Grateful for all that we are able to do through Him.

THE NEXT WORD I THINK OF IS **SELF-EXAMINATION**.

Paul, in his teachings concerning the Lord's Supper, says, *"A man should thoroughly examine himself, and only then should he eat the bread or drink the cup."* Without this honest searching, without this deeply probing look into the very center of my life, without this sincere self-examination, taking part in the Lord's Supper is empty and without meaning. It is completely void of any spiritual blessing or growth.

In the same letter to the Corinthians, Paul reminded them that careless Communion, without self-examination, means spiritual weakness.

So let us examine ourselves. When we do, God will become more real, communion with our Lord will be more vital, and our fellowship with other Christians will throb with a warm sense of togetherness.

110th Anniversary
First Baptist Church of Pulaski
August 13, 2006

I congratulate FBC on the celebration of the 110th anniversary of the church. Mary Lou and I rejoice with you on this historic occasion. I had the privilege of serving as pastor of the church for seventeen years, 1964-1981.

It has been 42 years since we first moved to Pulaski. A lot has happened, and the world has changed greatly during this time period. The computer age and rapidly changing technology have impacted our lives, our families, and even the way we "do" church.

Some of you have asked about my family. (Tell briefly about family.) Others have asked, "What are you doing now?" (Share this info.)

I have been asked to talk about the highlights of my tenure here. I preface these remarks by acknowledging that every pastor and staff person and every member of the congregation are to be commended today for the growth and accomplishments of the church. Paul said in 1 Corinthians 3, *"Who then is Paul and who is Apollos but ministers by whom ye believed?"* But he went on to say, *"Some plant, others water, but God gives the increase."*

Now, some highlights – time will not permit me to list all I remember, just a few:

1. Young couples were reached and added to the church. This was a key element in the growth of the church through those years.

Our Cradle Roll and Nursery programs were instrumental in facilitating the outreach and providing a teaching environment for babies and toddlers while parents attended Sunday School and worship.

2. The position of Minister of Music and Youth was added. This helped in the outreach of the church in two ways. The youth ministry provided a base to deepen the commitment of our current young people and to attract and win others. The music ministry was inspirational and added to the worship service. There was a youth choir, and youth ensembles were organized. New people were enlisted as a result.

3. Being the pastor of a large group of senior adults and ministering to their particular needs was a very rewarding part of my pastorate.

4. Steady growth in stewardship was evidenced, and missions giving in particular increased. This was gratifying.

5. Involvement in city and county life and activities brought blessings to me and the church.

6. Dr. Gerald Stow led in a great revival meeting that resulted in over 60 additions to the church. I baptized 49 people into the fellowship of FBC.

7. There were 3 county-wide crusades in Sam Davis Park that touched the lives of many throughout Giles County. The first crusade

was the largest religious gathering in the history of the county. There were over 4,500 in the final service. Dr. Stow led the first crusade; Dr. Bob Norman led the second meeting; and Dr. Stow, the third crusade.

8. I began a daily radio ministry over WKSR about midway of my pastorate here. It was called "The Pastor's Study" and was broadcast just before the 12 o'clock news. It featured music, interviews, devotions, and promotion of the church's ministry.

9. The seventeen years were a time of steadiness and commitment on the part of the members. We saw a maturing of faith and a stable congregation.

10. The Highland Baptist Mission that was begun by the church was organized as a church.

11. The church purchased additional property for parking.

12. Evangelism—reaching people for Christ—followed by equipping them for service in and through the church was a hallmark of those years.

Things I Have Learned as a Minister of the Gospel
Philippians 4:4-7, 10-13, 19 – 2 Timothy 4:1-5

INTRODUCTION

Today these remarks are based on God's Word, not to exalt anyone but Christ. What I share, I tell it in a spirit of humility, thanking God for allowing me to be His instrument in proclaiming the gospel of God.

On September 26, 1953 I was ordained to the ministry of the gospel in the Pollard Baptist Church of Ashland, Kentucky. It was a joyous occasion. It was a humbling experience. It was a moving, challenging time of my life. It was a time of questioning by the ordaining council.

During these 54 years I have served as an associate pastor, have had two seminary pastorates, four other pastorates (including Station Camp), eighteen interim pastorates, have been a hospital chaplain, have spent eight years as Partnership Mission Director of the Tennessee Baptist Convention, and have served twelve years as a Tennessee Baptist Children's Home consultant.

During this time I have: 1) proclaimed our great Baptist doctrines; 2) emphasized Southern Baptist Convention missions programs; 3) declared our rich Baptist heritage; 4) ministered to the needs of people; 5) comforted the bereaved in their sorrow; 6) set forth my vision of reaching people for Jesus Christ at home and abroad; 7) edified and built the local church, baptizing believers; 8) sounded the alarm when heresy was taught; 9) urged Christians to read God's Word; 10) encouraged the church to pray without ceasing; 11) stood tall against evil influence when I served as pastor; and 12) challenged the saints (the members of the church) to engage in the battle to win lost souls.

Paul's message to the Philippians and to Timothy helped me in my learning process:

Philippians –
        4:4 – Rejoice in God's goodness.
        4:11 – Be content.
        4:12 – I have had my ups and downs.
        4:13 – I have received strength.
        4:18 – My needs have been met.

2 Timothy –
        4:2 – Preach the Word. Reprove, rebuke, and exhort.
        4:3 – Make sure you preach sound doctrine to those who may turn away.
        4:5 – Watch yourself in all things, endure affliction, be an evangelist.
        4:5 – Carry out your ministry fully.

Now let me share some things I have learned. As I talk about these truths, let me say, "I am still learning." Also, as I set forth these things about ministry, apply them to your own heart and life.

I HAVE LEARNED THAT IT IS IMPORTANT TO BE IN THE WILL OF GOD.

Paul's ambition was to do God's will. He believed, as I do, that God has a purpose, a will, for each of us. I firmly believe that I was in His will in every situation in my ministry.

God has something for you to do in your life. Pray that you might find it.

I believe the Bible teaches that in the will of God there is contentment, security, and happiness.

I HAVE LEARNED THAT SUCCESS IN THE WORK OF THE CHURCH COMES THROUGH THE POWER OF THE HOLY SPIRIT.

It is not by might, not by manipulation, not through trickery, but by being energized by God's Spirit.

I HAVE LEARNED THAT THE HEADACHES, SORROWS, AND DISAPPOINTMENTS IN LIFE ARE GOD'S REAPPOINTMENTS TO GREATER USEFULNESS.

Paul says, in 2 Corinthians 12:7-10, *"I take pleasure in my difficult times for Christ's sake, for when I am weak, then I am strong."*

Romans 8:28 – *All things work together for good to those who love God and are called according to His purpose.*

This was true when I was diagnosed with cancer in my life. It can be true in your life.

I HAVE LEARNED THAT I MUST KEEP MY HEART AND MY LIFE RIGHT WITH GOD.

Satan is always working, stalking, and tempting. Using God's spiritual warfare has helped me be my best for Him. Being right with God also meant being right with others. What about you? As the hymn implores, "Is your heart right with God?"

Final Message
Station Camp Baptist Church
January 25, 2009

INTRODUCTION

my call

I was called to preach in March, 1950 and publicly dedicated my life to the ministry in April, 1950.

preparing

Tennessee Temple College, Chattanooga, 1950-53.

Pollard Baptist Church, Ashland, KY, May, 1953; served as associate pastor 8 months.

Ordained September, 1953. (Mary Lou found a church bulletin about that ordination while unpacking during our recent move.)

Southern Baptist Seminary, Louisville, KY, January 1954-May 1957

influences on my ministry

Thanks to my wonderful wife, Mary Lou, and our four children—Susan, Randy, Karen, and Scott—and their families for the encouragement and loyal support they have given me all the way.

My dear mother, Pauline, had a tremendous influence on my life, and I often told her so. I am grateful to my former pastors who mentored me and to the teachers who molded me. I am, most of all, thankful to God who called me and has guided me on my journey of 56 years in the ministry. This has included:

2 pastorates while in seminary; 4 full-time churches; four years as hospital chaplain; 7 years as Partnership Missions Director, TBC; 10 years as consultant for Tennessee Baptist Children's Homes; and interim pastor for 18 churches in Middle Tennessee.

This also includes, of course, the last 40 months in this historic church. I truly thank the people of Station Camp Baptist Church for the joy of serving here: Johnny Keene and the pastor search committee; our teachers, officers, and committee members; Bobby Gammon, Ricky Suter, and the Station Camp Gospel Choir; the ladies who have served on the kitchen committee, preparing for events such as today; and to all the members who have attended, prayed, and been involved in this church they love.

A special word of appreciation is due to godly pastors who have served this church for 212 years. Because of their leadership, the church is alive and well today.

GOD IS GOOD (Nahum 1:7)

The prophet Nahum, in 1:7, penned these words:

God is good. He is a stronghold in time of need, and He knows those who trust in Him.

I can testify to that truth. Throughout my ministry, God has been gracious and good. He has been a stronghold for me in all the joys and hurts of a ministry of 56 years. As already noted, God has been good to Station Camp Baptist Church from 1796 to the present. In my forty months as your pastor, I have seen evidences of His goodness to us. Because of His blessings to us, I feel good about the following:

- We have a warm, loving fellowship of believers.

- You are receptive to the preaching of His Word.

- Our Sunday School has grown through new classes added.

- People have been saved and baptized.

- New families have moved their membership here.

- The sanctuary has been updated with new window treatments.

- We have seen the renovation of the nursery classroom by Darcy and Cary Vinson and the addition of a nursery during worship services.

- The Garrison building has been renovated for use by the youth of the church.

- The music ministry has grown under the leadership of Bobby Gammon and Ricky Suter. The Station Camp Gospel Choir is a real blessing to the church and others.

- There has been an increase in the giving of tithes and offerings. I feel especially good about the increased gifts to foreign and home missions

- Yes, God has blessed us with many things to feel good about. I feel good about the future of this church. It is as bright as the promises of God.

A GOOD WORD (Proverbs 25:11)

A word fitly spoken (or *"spoken in the right circumstance"*) *is like apples of gold in settings of silver.*

Using the words of the wisdom writer, allow me to challenge you to say words of love, thanks, and encouragement in the church, in your home, and in your relationship with others. These words are a small investment, often spoken in a few seconds, but they can bestow a blessing that will linger a lifetime. When sincerely spoken, they are like oil in machinery that keeps down friction.

P.S.

About 15 years ago, I received some promotional material from the Foreign Mission Board of the SBC. It was a very interesting article entitled, "What We Need in Our Churches is P.S." P.S., in letter-writing, means "postscript" or afterthought, something added to the letter. But P.S. here means "Prayer Support". Colossians 4:3 – *"Praying also for us."* 2 Thessalonians 3:1 – *"Pray for us."*

Prayer Support is **vital**.

Prayer Support is **important**.

Prayer Support is **exciting**. As you pray, you can see God work in unexpected ways.

Prayer Support means **victories won** and **a time to rejoice**.

Prayer Support is **effective** – it gets the job done. James wrote, *"The effectual fervent prayer of a righteous man availeth much."*

Prayer Support is **exacting**. It is not easy, not simple, not cheap. Prayer support is hard. You must make time to pray. Pray without ceasing! It has to be a priority.

Prayer Support is **essential.** Jesus said, *"You have not because you ask not."* Praying is the lifeblood of a Christian and the church.

I Prayed
Gwen McLendon Day

> I prayed – and the loads were lifted;
> I prayed – and the storms were stilled;
> I prayed – and hands were strengthened,
> Feet were guided, needs were filled.
>
> I prayed – and doors were opened;
> I prayed – and work was done;
> I prayed – and hearts were melted,
> Lives were changed and souls were won.
>
> I prayed – and God responded.
> His miracles were everywhere;
> The church was blessed, the Kingdom
>   hastened;
> What power lies within prayer!

NOW ALL TOGETHER

My final word today comes from the book of Judges, from an incident in the life of Gideon. People called Midianites had defeated Israel and taken many captive, and God raised up Gideon to rescue the nation. Gideon followed God's plan to the letter, although it was an unusual one. The Midianite army was large, and Gideon's followers initially numbered about 22,000. But God told Gideon to reduce that number—first to 10,000, then eventually to only 300—and these were to be divided further into three camps of 100 each as they went against the enemy.

For the nighttime battle, each man was given a lit torch, a trumpet, and an empty pitcher. Gideon then instructed them, *"Hide your lights under the pitchers. When I blow my trumpet, you blow your trumpets and shout, 'The sword and the Lord and Gideon!' Then smash your pitchers."*

That night, as they crept around the Midianite camp:

- **All together** they blew their trumpets.

- **All together** they smashed the pitchers.

- **All together** 300 torches were blazing, lighting the camp.

- **All together** they shouted, *"The sword and the Lord and Gideon!"*

The frightened Midianites began fighting each other and started fleeing. A great victory was won because the Israelites were **all together**.

This is the message I share with you now. Do you want God's blessing on the church? Do you want growth in the church? Then **all together**:

-PRAY-

-WORK-

-SHOW CHRISTIAN LOVE-

MOVE FORWARD
ALL TOGETHER
IN THE MINISTRY OF THE CHRUCH
AND THE KINGDOM OF GOD

AFTERWORD

I accepted Jesus as my Savior at the age of 9. It was March 16, 1975 and I will never forget it. My father was soon to turn 49 and he had been the pastor at First Baptist Church Pulaski for almost 11 years. He had been an ordained minister for more than 30 years. I had lived my life in church. From my 9-year-old perspective it was just like school and home, it was somewhere else I went to — a lot. The people there were, and many still are, like my family. I sat in those pews hundreds of times. I played, drew and slept through many of my Dad's sermons. One time they even left me asleep at church, something I still get asked about to this day.

I can't tell you which sermon he preached that day, but I can tell you that I wasn't sleeping, playing or drawing. God had my full attention. It wasn't the words being spoken, but the message God had for me. It was time, right now. His Son's gift was for me that day.

When the invitation was offered that Sunday morning I squirmed in my seat as God pulled on my heart, until I couldn't sit there a second longer. When I started down the aisle it was about the Father, the Son, and the Holy Spirit and their business with me. My heart was about to jump out of my chest; I was overcome with joy. Everything past, present and future was right at that moment. It's a feeling only those who have accepted Jesus' gift will ever know. It's a feeling I strongly urge you to seek out if you haven't. I'm sitting here 40 years later and, despite all the things I've done to damage my relationship with God, I still feel what that 9-year-old boy felt when he started down that aisle. God wants you to feel it.

But something happened that changed my experience. It was something that, when you think of how many people have lived since Jesus died on the cross, has been experienced by relatively few. As I walked down that aisle full of happiness, ready to accept the gift I couldn't earn and never deserved, I realized that God's servant waiting for me at the altar was my father. It was the first time I really saw my father as the man of God he is and as the messenger of God he is. About halfway down the aisle our eyes met and we both burst into tears. I believe there was so much joy that day between father and son that our bodies couldn't hold it all in and it started flowing out of us in our tears. That memory is as vivid for me today as it was the day it happened.

Millions of people have accepted Jesus as their Savior and many of those are amazing stories of inspiration, love, mercy and grace. Each person's experience in accepting Jesus is different and special, but I wouldn't trade mine for any of them.

I saw my Dad in a different light after that. I watched him minister to the grieving, the lonely, the poor, the hopeless, the lost and the saved. People called our home and my Dad was there for them. I was with him when people would stop him and ask for prayers. He has literally traveled around the world and shared the love of Jesus Christ — and he's my Dad!

After he left the ministry at First Baptist Church Pulaski I didn't get to hear my father preach as much. As we moved on in our lives, I didn't get to see the difference he made in people's lives as much. We played golf. We watched football and basketball together. We laughed. We cried. We loved. We have lived the life of a father and son on earth. Our relationship has always been amazing, but I stopped seeing my father as the servant of God he is.

As I typed in some of the sermons for this book over the past few months, I started to see my father again in the light of his ministry. I saw his life reflected in his words and his love for all of God's children in the sermons he preached. I became that 9-year-old boy again, in the midst of accepting Jesus as my Savior and seeing my father at the altar ready to shepherd me into God's loving arms. I was reminded again of the blessing God gave me to be the son of one of His chosen messengers.

When you grow up a pastor's child it's different. Not bad, just different. You don't even realize it. He's just your Dad until one day God shows you what he really is. These 56 sermons from my Dad's ministry are a glimpse of a man — a husband, a father, a son and a messenger of God.

A couple of notes.

• I started thinking a couple of years ago about getting Dad's sermons typed up for him just so he would know they would be preserved. Last Christmas I mentioned it to Randy and this book was started. Thanks to Randy, Susan and Mom for their work on it, especially Randy, who did most of it.

• I think my Dad will be the first to tell you that not a single one of these sermons, nor his ministry, would have been possible without Mary Lou Stewart. She'll probably wish that wasn't in here.

• My Dad had a lot of sayings. Anyone who heard him preach should remember a couple of them:

"Young people are you listening?"

"That's the first mistake I've made today."

My favorite, however, was "I like that."

I'm pretty sure that's what he'll say when he sees this book.

Love you Dad,
Scott

*You therefore, my son,
be strong in the grace
that is in Christ Jesus.*
2 Timothy 2:1